Generation You

THE AWAKENING HAS BEGUN

An Interactive Experience

Rick Dorociak

the PeppertreePress

Sarasota, Florida

www.RickDorociak.com

ISBN: 978-1-61493-520-9

Library of Congress Number: 2017909545

Printed August 2017

It's time to break free
from all the daily stresses
and finally start living the life
you have always imagined.

In memory of
Your Past

and

Dedicated to
This Moment

**Before you begin this book, I have three questions
for you. They pertain to where you are at in your life.
This may very well be the most important page
you read in this book, so here we go...**

QUESTION 1. What do you think is the main reason that
you are not living your dreams?

_____

_____

_____

QUESTION 2. What would it take to get you where you
want to be in life?

_____

_____

_____

QUESTION 3. What are you willing to do to get there?

_____

_____

_____

_____

These three questions were created to help you understand where you are in life and what it will take to start making the necessary changes to live the most amazing life possible. Just take out a piece of paper, write these questions down and answer them. Remember, this is YOUR life that you are answering questions about. If you don't take them seriously, who will?

Answering these three specific questions is the beginning of a life changing experience for you. I have spoken to many people on the subject of living the life they have always imagined and it is *these* questions that have put them on the path to change. Once you answer them (honestly) you can then expand on what needs to be done. I cannot stress enough that small changes will make BIG impacts. When you have finished reading this book I want you to ask yourself these three questions again, and once again, answer them honestly. Let's see if you change any of your answers.

I am so excited for all the possibilities that are before you. I love nothing better than seeing people start to live the most amazing lives they can! Therefore, if you have answered the three questions, then it is time to proceed and I welcome you to all that is possible...

First Things First . . .

As you begin this book, I want to get a few things out of the way. First, you are going to read the word "God" throughout this book. I understand that many people have different belief systems. Some may choose the word God to refer to what they believe in, while others may use words such as: The Creator, The Universe, Mother Earth, World Spirit, Life Force, Absolute Being, Alpha & Omega, etc. Whatever you choose to call whatever it is you believe in, know that this book is being written from the perspective of universal love. All are welcome to choose their own set of beliefs. This is just my perspective.

Secondly, this book only works if you are willing to believe not just in this book, but also in yourself. **You** are the biggest part to changing your life. Next, this is not a magical book that when you read it everything you have ever wished for just suddenly appears. Changing your life will take some effort on your part. Finally, know that God (the universe) is, was, and always will be part of your life. Think not? Then think again. It does not matter if you have found that spiritual connection with Him in your existence or not, because we are all in a perpetual state of God (universal love).

The ideas and stories within the pages of this book mostly pertain to my life and how spiritual and positive thinking have changed it. Throughout the pages there may be a few stories from other people's lives, but in most cases the stories are based on my own life experiences. Keeping that in mind, you will have your own life experiences once you have read this book and put in the effort necessary to do so. This book *can be* life changing if you allow it to be, but it is up to you to make that choice.

Also, all of us have some sort of baggage we are carrying around on a daily basis. This baggage is usually from our past and does not need to be part of our future. Here is my advice to you, drop the bags and move on. I cannot say it any simpler than that. Since you are taking the next steps in your journey of self-discovery, the bags have to stop here. If you are ready to drop them and continue on, then let's begin the next phase of your spiritual exploration.

Faith, Hope, & Belief

The three most important words in any language

Serenity

Serenity abounds in all those who are traveling the true path of enlightenment. Where are you now in your travels? The knack of finding your true treasures within yourself is not complicated. Human beings seem to make everything a little more complex than it needs to be. To travel the journey of self-fulfillment will take you to places that you have never been to before or even thought were possible. The secret to finding this is to look deep within your own consciousness. It is waiting to be found. Just as a baby bird must look deep within himself to take that first gesture towards flight, you must do the same. The search begins in your soul.

The mysteriousness of one's own soul is not a mystery at all to those who have found it and have thus transformed their lives. This gift (the soul) is the beginning of where our travels embark. It is through your soul that you are brought to a higher level of awareness. It is also through your soul that you first experience the gift of life. For you to experience even a single moment of your soul is enough to bring your life to a higher level of clarity. Your spirituality will be heightened, thus bringing you closer to God and realizing your oneness with Him and all that is, was, and ever will be.

The time is now for you to experience all the joys and wonders that await you on your own exploration of the inner workings of your mysticism. The experiences that you will have will make your journey like none you have ever imagined before. Along the way you will learn the meaning of your life, and you will be able to understand where the plan will take you. The idea of living the most amazing life is sometimes the journey itself. To be taken to the most outer limits of one's own sense of reality can only be explained by those who have been there. To go where only God has gone before is a journey few will ever take. However, you are about to join those few.

Sit back, relax, and take a deep breath. You have just begun the journey of a lifetime – your lifetime. Enjoy the trip.

God is love. Love is God.

DEVOTION BEFORE WE BEGIN . . .

Beloved God, we know that freedom is one of the greatest gifts you have ever bestowed upon us. The feeling of complete sovereignty within the realm of our own being is unlike any other that we will ever know. We also know that there is nobody to stand in judgment of us, and it is a miraculous sensation that all of us need to appreciate. To know individually that we are at peace with all that is right in the world is a joy that we shall not take for granted. We thank you for a mind that is clear and ready for everything that is before us. We understand our place in humanity and we know that no egos shall contend with the love you have for all of us. We also know that your love knows no boundaries. Your gift of freedom will flourish within the imagination of all of us. We will live life with no abandon because of you. We take pleasure in life and shall live it for all it is worth spiritually, physically, and mentally. It was through you that we were created in the image of universal love and we thank you for this gift. To all our brothers and sisters around the world we only wish peace, health, and happiness forever and ever. Thank you God for these gifts of personal freedom and all they entail.

Peace, Joy, Love & Abundance to all.

Love only knows love

ONE'S TRUE DESTINY . . .

What a great day to be alive! A day filled with the unlimited potential that anything is possible. Today dreams will come true; hopes will be realized, and desires will be fulfilled. Effective immediately, God has opened the doors to everything that you could ever imagine. Today is your day to take charge of all the things, big or small, that you have been waiting to let loose upon. What are you waiting for? Today *is* the day!

At one time or another, you have all lived in the world of "someday". You say "someday" this will happen or "someday" that will happen, but in reality it never will. The reason for this is that "someday" does not exist. You need to live every second of everyday. Do not let any breath go without notice. You need to realize the significance of this if you want to experience all that your life has to offer. You have been given the opportunity to be the person that you have always known you would be. Who that person is, is up to you. Nobody can tell you who you are, but you. You are in control of your destiny. You and only you can decide what that destiny will be.

Each choice you make leads you on a new path of life. Sometimes you choose the wrong path, but maybe it has been the right path all along. Does right or wrong even exist? In any event, you have been given the gift of change. You have been given the actual ability to change your life at any given moment. Each moment should be special, and it should be celebrated. It should be a reflection of who you are. To reach this place, you must look within yourself to find the real you. This is the "you" that exists within your soul. The real you who is one with God.

Your soul contains everything about you. It is literally who and what you are. It holds all the answers to all the questions of life. Look deep within yourself and you will find it. Trust me – you will know when you have made that connection. Once you have and you are one with your soul, you will unlock another door to your future – a door overflowing with all that is obtainable. A door that once opened, will create the person you were meant to be. Live life in abundance, and never give up on what will one day come to realization, that you are one with everything that is, was and ever will be. In the end, this is one's true destiny.

Without the first step, no journey can begin.

POP QUIZ (HINT, YES)

My friend, I have a few questions I would like to ask you before we continue. Please circle the appropriate answer to each question (and be honest).

I am reading this book because it's time for ME?	Yes	No
I can be whoever I want to be?	Yes	No
I can do whatever I want to do in life?	Yes	No
I will make changes in my life starting today?	Yes	No
I serve a greater purpose in life?	Yes	No
I promise to read this entire book?	Yes	No
The answer to each question is yes?	Yes	No

Of course the answer to each question is yes. You obviously, like millions of others, are looking to enhance your life. Whether it is spiritual, emotional, or physical, all of us are continuously searching for better ways to improve the way we live. Here is where this book comes into play. God is telling you to go ahead and be you. You were born with a soul, and a purpose. Your purpose is to be who you desire to be, to do what you desire to do, and to connect with other people in the process who are looking for the same things.

This is the wonderful gift about life. We are all given the opportunity daily to experience great things within ourselves and the world around us. Yes, there are a lot of problems in the world, but we are not going to be able to help anyone if we are not where we desire to be at in life.

Each day is a new day for you to learn the skills and knowledge necessary to achieve all that is before you. Through these everyday encounters with your very own existence you are able to achieve a sense of well being within your own life. It's time to reward yourself for a job well done. You have come this far, so now it is time to take your life to an entirely new level. A level of such intensity, that you would have never thought in your wildest dreams that you could have ever reached it. Feel secure in who and what you are. Know that God is with you at all times, and that He loves you unconditionally. We all have areas in our lives that could use a little tweaking. In fact, I had a lot of areas in my own life that I needed to tear down completely and rebuild from the ground up; but this is a great gift from God, the universe. You have been given the actual ability to make modifications within your own life if you choose to do so. Yes, there it is, the word *choose*. You need to *choose* to do it. And you can! Thoughts without actions are meaningless.

The messages in this book are here to help you explore a few things about yourself that you probably never knew before. Just like my last book, *Taking Care of God,* taught people about the four core parts of your soul and the answer to the million-dollar question, *Generation You* is going to do the same. You are going to learn about something called the M.S.C. (you will find out later what that stands for), and you will also learn more about your soul, meditation, healing, and the benefits of relaxation. You will learn to use words such as, *outstanding* and *prominent* when speaking about yourself and others. We are leaving the negatives at the door and heading to positive town.

I want you to feel good about yourself as you start to come across parts of your own life that you never knew existed. Those are the parts that are connected to your soul and all that it has to offer. Spirituality is very important in everyone's life, and it will soon become second nature in your life too. If you have never tapped into your own spirituality, you will, and you are going to be so happy that you did. If you are somebody who is already on this journey and you have experienced your own spirituality, then this will take you to an even deeper level of your own consciousness. Know that I can sense the excitement already building up within you. As it grows, so do you as a person. Feeling good about who you are is an immense stress reliever.

Therefore, I want you to enjoy all the information you are about to receive, but more importantly I want you to enjoy life. Stay positive on your continuing journey of self-realization and know that I sometimes get a little repetitive when I write. That is only because I try and make sure that people understand how significant certain areas are. Everything in life is vital to your very existence, and now it is time to start enjoying what God and you have created. Once you have decided to make some changes in your life, know that you have already begun your new journey. So sit back and be comfortable as you continue on your journey of self-discovery. By the way, by reading this book your change has already begun. Congratulations!

One cannot be where one should be at in life, if one does not know where one even is.

Shake It Up

When I wrote my last book, *Taking Care of God: The Soul Purpose of Life,* I never intended or even thought that I would write a follow up book to it. However, God has placed it in my heart to keep the momentum going. So here it is, the next moment of spiritual happiness in life.

Let's get right into it. Let me ask you, what changes have you made in your life in the last few weeks that were for the positive? Have you made any changes at all? In the beginning, I believe it is essential to address where you are at in your journey of self-discovery, while you continue to learn more about who you are spiritually. If you are as excited as I am, then let's head off into that vast new world that you are creating for yourself and discover even more.

Maybe you have made some small changes within your life, but you are still not quite sure where you are heading just yet. Now what do you do? Do you continue on the same path you're on or do you dare to move in an entirely new direction? The answer to this question is simple. You need to venture off into whatever you feel is the right path for you. However, as my friend Neal Donald Walsh has said, "life begins at the end of your comfort zone," so try something new. Chances are you have become complacent in your own comfort zone. It is time to take control and start creating new and exciting ideas for your life. Most people who are starting to put their lives back together or those that are just starting to reap the benefits from making new changes in it, are far to often afraid to step out from their newly created existence. They once again become stuck in their comfort zone. "Generation You" is all about stepping out of that zone and into the unknown.

Let's take the path you have created for you and shake it up a little bit. We are going to work together on creating new and exciting experiences for all of us. I am also on this journey; it is never ending, so you are not alone. Don't forget that God, the universe, is with you at all times too.

Everything you are reading right now is because God opened a new door in my life and yours. He wanted me to share these new experiences with you personally. He wants you to know that He did not create your life strictly to live day to day, but to live moment to moment. Although we are hear to work towards helping humanity and serving each other, we are also supposed to enjoy the benefits that God, the universe, has created for us.

Therefore, what can we do to start enjoying all those benefits? There are a lot of things, and we are going to go over many in this book; but I need you to promise me that you will take what you read to heart. This book is not being written so I can just simply type words on a page. No, this book is about you. The words are merely a way to inform you all of the great things that life have in store for you, if you choose to act upon them. So start acting!

SECTION ONE

YOU...

This is the only section of the book,
because this book is all about you.

Remember there are no chapters in this book,
because we live our lives in moments
and not chapters.

Enjoy...

WE ALL SHARE A COMMON SPIRITUAL BOND...

Let's start with the basic fundamentals of spirituality. Who or what is God? Saying that God is the Spiritual network that connects all things can sum up who He is. Some may call him *God* (like me), while others may call him *The Universe, The Creator, The Source* or whatever name they choose. However, in the end we are all associated with one another through this divine connection. Because of this divine connection, we all have something else in common. What is this common factor? It is the ability of infinity. We all have the ability to live forever through our souls. But what is the soul? The soul is the epicenter of who we are as a being. In *Taking Care of God,* I broke down the four core parts of the soul to its basic nature. To refresh some minds, the four core parts are: consciousness, origin, reality, and eternity. These four C.O.R.E parts make up who we are.

The soul was designed by God to put balance into your life. What you see before you (reality) is only a mere picture of what you are creating for yourself. It is a manifestation of your own independent thought, a reflection of what you are sending out into the universe. In a simpler term, it is your thoughts that you have put into action. If you do not like what you are seeing, then change the reflection. Know that everyone has a spiritual bond between one another, but what you see as your reality is not what others may see as theirs.

Through harmonic focal points in our bodies, we are able to create health and balance within ourselves. The body contains seven of those focal points called Chakras. The seven Chakras are: Root, Sexual, Solar Plexus, Heart, Throat, Third Eye, and Crown. These are points of energy within our bodies. Everything about us as human beings is energy and vibrations. These vibrational patterns form all that you see. From there you must also understand that we as human beings are also made up of masculine and feminine qualities. The dualities of both of these parts help to define us as a person. As we grow in the womb, some of us will take on a more feminine quality (becoming women) and others a more masculine quality (becoming men), but we maintain both qualities within us.

As we continue our study into our own spirituality, we will also find information pertaining to God in almost every religion. These religions will also go on to say that we were all created by God, therefore making us all one with each other. These religions will also tell us that we need to maintain a relationship with God. I see this as our true connection to all things past, present, and future. Building a relationship with God is building a relationship with us. For any relationship to exist it must have love as its founding basis, and I am sure you would agree with this. As for a religion, I do not follow any of them per se'. What I choose to follow may not be what you choose to follow. You will have your own path to God.

Continue on your spiritual journey, and discover all that is possible within you. Do not forget who you are or where you came from. Use this knowledge to live the best life possible. Remember, your dreams are only a thought away.

Change just one thing about you right now, and you have changed your reality.

SUBJECT TO CHANGE

In life, all things are subject to change. There is nothing on this planet that will not at some point endure a number of transformations within itself. Whether that change is physical, psychological, or spiritual, change is constant. We, as humans, are in a never-ending state of change. Every moment of everyday, we are making some type of modification to ourselves. Some changes may be so subtle that we do not even recognize them, while other changes may be so great that we feel or see a significant shift in who we are as a being.

Understand that change is a good thing. This means that you are evolving into the person you were meant to be. Along with these changes, you have the capability to modify any variations that are made to you or by you. You will find that a simple adjustment may be all that is needed. At the same time though, you will realize that major transformations are the solutions. Changes are inherent to who you are as a living being. Not all changes made to you are by you. Some are the mere progression of life. Take the subject of growing older. Although, people try to stop the process, aging is just a fact of life, and everyone goes through it.

Do not be afraid or worried about change. The changes you are making within your life right now are being done to improve your way of life. Your changes may be small or great, but they are changes, and they will occur. With change comes even more change. Eventually you will notice that you may have completely reshaped your life. You have taken it from one point and shifted it to another, and by doing so you have now altered the course of your destiny. You are reshaping what your destiny will entail, and only you can change whatever that is. Outside forces may change you, but you have the ability to stay on track in your journey of self-discovery. It is up to you to keep the changes that are being made in your life or to alter them to complete your fate. In other words, your destiny is waiting for you, but is subject to change, by you. Let's start those changes…

Open your mind to a new way of thinking and in the process open new destinations for your life.

THE CROSSROADS

What is your place in the universe? Who are you really? Do you know? Should you know? Life can bring up so many questions, and you may have no answers to them. Then again, maybe you do and you just haven't found them yet.

Created by God, we all have been chosen at this exact moment to live what God had planned to be the most magnificent life possible. However, due to some unforeseen circumstances, and some that we have placed before ourselves, we have not lived life as we should have. As we continue on this journey called life, we continue to seek out the answers needed to live the most astonishing lives that God has created. Where do we go from here? What is next? What do we do?

Now is the time to take a chance on life and start to live. God has placed it in our hearts that we are only here for a short amount of time. Sixty, seventy or even eighty years is nothing compared to eternity. What we choose to do with this time is up to us. Know that the past is the past, and only this moment is what remains. We can choose to live in the moment, or we can choose to let the moments pass us by. Either way, we are in control of what is before us. Now is the time to make the choice.

I would think that the choice would be easy for most, but I know some of you are not comfortable with change. Let me put it another way. What is a more comfortable way to live? Living a life that is going nowhere, or living one that is filled with all of your dreams and adventures coming into play? The choice is yours. I am not here to make the decision for you, but to let you know what is next when you take on the challenge of life and live it to its fullest. The entire world is at your disposal. You can be and do whatever it is you desire, but only if you choose to make it a reality.

Here you stand at what I would call the crossroads of your life. There are two choices at these crossroads. The choices are to continue your current path or to head in the direction of a new life surrounded by all that is possible. You have to make the decision on which road you take. Time is ticking away as you sit there and think. Each second that ticks away is a second that you do not get back and is lost forever. Do you know what forever is? Forever is endless time. It is what exists directly before you.

You do not want to look back on your life and think to yourself that you could have done this or should have done that, knowing that you had ample opportunities to do so, and never took them. I know that this is not how I want to live. I want to live life to its fullest. I want to be able to do whatever it is I want to do whenever I want to do it. I can only do that by taking complete control of my life and just doing it.

I have seen so many of my friends and family members leave this world, and most of them never lived the most wonderful lives they could have. All they had at the end were memories of what could have been. I don't want to leave this world with what could have been. Do you? I want to leave this world and transition knowing that I lived life for all it was worth.

Here it is – choice time. You can sit and read this book hoping your life will change, or you can read this book and start putting it into action, and live the life you were destined to live; the life that God and you created together. This choice is yours. What is it going to be? Do you turn the page and take control? I believe with all my heart that you will make the right decision. Once you do, life as you know will cease to exist, and the life you have always longed for will begin. You are at the crossroads; it is time to decide.

The time is now

GENERATION YOU

Welcome my friends to your new life of abundance, and what I call "Generation You: The Awakening Has Begun." It is not the next generation; it is the generation of NOW. It is the generation of those who live in each and every moment. If you are reading this book, then you are part of it. Generation You knows no age, gender, race, ethnicity, sexual orientation or religion. It is the generation of those who already know they can have or be anything they choose to be by simply knowing that it already exists within in their lives; they can control their own destiny. Generation You is the generation that makes the final decision on which direction to take. In this generation it is you who creates the abundance, and it is you who knows how to get that abundance. It is you! Yes, it is you!

At this moment you have the ability to choose at any time what your future will entail. As a part of Generation You, thoughts become dreams and dreams become realities. No more just getting by. In the simplest of terms, you now control what you will and will not have in your life. Throughout history many have been a part of this generation, yet so few have acted upon it. Do you want to be famous or wealthy? If so, you have to know that you already are. Do not just imagine driving that new car; know that you already own it. The power of thought is amazing. What do you think drives the human race? The answer is thought. Those that are the happiest in the world know the power that Generation You holds. Although everybody has the same opportunities, only a mere few ever take the steps to realize the power of thought. Those who do not act upon it will never understand the power they possess until they finally realize this gift from God. Who has the power? Everyone does.

Your thoughts provoke your mind to react. That reaction is what creates realities. The power of thought controls every aspect of your life. From when you get up in the morning to when you smile. It is even controlling when you would read this book. Whatever you think about, your mind and body reacts to it and takes you in that direction. If you think about negatives, your mind creates them, and you constantly run into obstacles. If you think you are poor, then all you will be is poor. If you think you are wealthy, then your mind works with you to create a lifestyle of wealth.

You need to know how powerful the mind is and "Generation You" knows this. The difference between most people and "Generation You" is the fact that "Generation You" understands the power it has to create its own destiny. Once you realize that you have this same power, your life will start to change right before your eyes. You will see things that you once thought would never come into your life, start to materialize. Know the world is yours, and in time it will be. To use this power to the best of its ability, you need to visualize everything. If you want that brand new car, you need to see yourself driving it. What color is it? Convertible or hardtop? Automatic or stick shift? Leather wrapped steering wheel or not? You need to position yourself in the vehicle. You need to see yourself driving it all the time. You must do this in order for your thoughts to materialize. The more you think about it, the faster those things will come into your life.

Here is the key to unlocking your destiny and all that it will possess. One word, "know", can change your life instantly. "Generation You" understands the key of "knowing", and that is why "Generation You" controls its own destiny – because "Generation You" knows and now you know too. Take a stand for your generation, *Generation You,* and know!

Never underestimate the healing power of happiness!

Miracles

Miracle this and miracle that; everyone receives miracles and that's a fact! Having a little fun, but it's the truth! When most people think about miracles it's usually when they are in a situation of dire need. Whether it is health, finances or even relationship troubles, this is when most people always seem to ask or pray for a miracle to happen in their life or someone else's. When in all actuality the Universe is in a constant state of miracles. Not one moment goes by without the Universe providing miracles all over our planet.

So, what is a miracle? Well the dictionary defines it as this: an effect or extraordinary event in the physical world that surpasses all known human or natural powers and is ascribed to a supernatural cause. Would you agree? Okay, so these "events" happen all the time. We as humans have been taught over the years to only see miracles at certain times, such as the ones described earlier. Once again, miracles are a constant within all of our lives. Now I am sure many of you are saying that you may be leading a rough life right now or something is seriously wrong and nothing has happened to change it. Well the problem is we lock our definition of what a miracle is into the textbook definition of one.

Think about your everyday life. We all take for granted everything within it. The fact that we got up this morning to me is always a miracle. Not because we're not sick or injured, but because life is not a given. I always tell people that the obituary column in the daily paper is filled with people who thought they had another day. What I mean by that is every day we are alive needs to be looked at as a "gift" not as a "given". A roof over our heads, food on the table, family or friends, these are all miracles. Once against most of us take these things for granted. Everything I just mentioned (family, friends and so forth) I have lost at one time or another in my life. Therefore, I do not take anything or anyone within my life for granted; they are all miracles to me.

Miracles are a matter of perspective. It is how we see things that make them miracles. As for the expectations of miracles for things like sickness or money and so forth, well yes, expect them, because the Universe is always at work creating miracles every moment of every day. The key is to believe in them.

Love your life,
live your dreams,
never live in fear
and always believe in miracles...

Small changes bring BIG opportunities

THE SNOWFLAKE

I can remember growing up as a child in the suburbs of Chicago and every winter playing in the freshly fallen snow with my friends. I couldn't wait to get out there and build snow-forts and have snowball fights with them. Looking back, I never realized how amazing that snow really was. It is made up of billions of tiny ice crystals known as snowflakes. Snowflakes are so intricate, and no two are the same. The same goes for you as a person; you are not like anybody else. You are the only one of you.

You need to understand the power of God, and the fact that He has the infinite ability to make each one of us different. Although God made all of us, we are all distinctive in our own right. We may have some of the same features as our family members, but even twins differ from each other. Yes, identical twins are not identical in all aspects. That's what makes us unique. The fact remains that there are billions of people on this planet and no two of us are alike.

You need to know how important you are as an individual. You need to understand that God made all of us to Universal satisfaction. He gave all of us the ability to be who we desire to be as human beings. You have the power to be you, and you can be anything you want to be in life. God has given you the power to make decisions about the direction you would like your life to follow. However, there is a catch to this and here it is. You must recognize the fact that you have to live with your decisions.

Sometimes that seems to be the hardest part of decision making, living with the consequences of them.

You have the capability to be and do whatever you feel is right for your life. Remember your actions today directly affect those around you, so when making those decisions, make them wisely. Know that God (the universe) has placed you here at this exact moment for a reason. You are right where you are supposed to be, because you are meant to do something great with your life, and it is up to you to find out what that is. Through your quest of finding yourself spiritually, I am sure you have noticed, like a snowflake, those little intricacies that make up who you are as a person. Those details, no matter how small, make up your very existence.

Now I ask this question, who are you? Do you know yet or are you still searching for the answer? Over time, we eventually find the answer to the question of who we are. Some may find the answer rather quickly, while others like me found out forty plus years into life. It does not matter when you find the answer; it's that you continually seek the answer to the question. Dare to be different in your life. Don't conform to some cookie cutter way of existence. This is not what God intended for you. God intended for you to be different when He created you. He created you, once again, to be you.

Seek the answers to your life by finding them deep within yourself. All the answers you seek are waiting to be found in your soul. Your soul is the key to your very way of life. Unlike the snowflake, God has given you a soul and has entrusted you with the ability to seek it out and find your true path. We all have a destiny in life, but each destiny is different. Just as you are as diverse from each other, so is the path that each of you is taking. Each one of us has our own trail to blaze in life. As an example of this let's use the snowflake again. Each snowflake travels its own individual route to its final destination. No two snowflakes will ever take the same exact path. Although their eventual outcome is the same, their journey will never be identical. You are the same way. No two people will ever take the same exact path to their destiny. Although, you may have common goals with others and may follow similar paths, each one will be different.

Understand that you are like no other person on the planet. This is essential in your pursuit of self-awareness and will help guide you on your quest to find the real you deep within yourself. The fact that God (the universe) has made you exactly as you are is enough to know that you are a special person in the greater scheme of things. He wants you to enjoy all the privileges of being created by love, but in doing so, He wants you to know that you are an individual and you have the right to make your own decisions in life (freewill). Although He will guide you, it is up to you to make the final decisions. Next, what decisions have you made so far? Are you heading on the correct path? Only you can answer that question. Remember everyone has different paths in life. The one you choose today may not be the one you are on tomorrow. This is due to your ever-changing perspectives.

Unlike us, the snowflake is guided by atmospheric conditions that are out of its control. We on the other hand have control of the direction we take, to a point. Thanks to our ever-changing perspective, we have the ability to see things and immediately change our course of direction. By doing this we change our outcome. God has given us the ability to change anything in a single moment. Anything we are doing right now, we can change right now. Take this book for example. If I choose, I can start writing about anything I want. However, I choose to write what I am writing right now. The same goes for anything in life. You can choose to change at any moment, and in turn change the course of your life. Once again, with every change you make, you are changing your circumstances and your perspective, and in doing so you alter the direction of your life. I am not saying that this is a bad thing, because many times it has to be done in order for you to achieve your destiny. Remember, for every change there is a consequence, and for every consequence there is a change. You must keep this in mind when you are changing things within your life.

To give you a visual example of this, let us use our friend the snowflake again. The snowflake is falling gently to the earth when all of a sudden the wind picks up speed and changes direction. This now changes the course of the snowflake. In turn, the snowflake now falls into a vast pile of snowflakes already on a busy road. The accumulation of those snowflakes now causes a large pile of snow to build up along the roadway causing road closures and delays. Here is the breakdown. The snowflake is you; the change is the wind, and the consequence is the large build-up of snow on the road. That build-up or consequence has caused drivers to change their path to a different destination. Needless to say, every change causes a consequence, and every consequence causes a change.

When deciding which direction to take in life, it is important to see the big picture. Know ahead of time what each change will bring. This way you are prepared for the consequences of those actions. You already know what you need to do to continue on your journey of spiritual happiness. We are all on this journey together, so let's look out for one another. Now let's head into an entirely new area of your life – the area of the unexpected...

Once you start to believe that life has beaten you, it is up to you to decide if you are down for the count.

VEER OFF THE BEATEN PATH

Please stop it! Stop it right now! Stop living your life in the same cramped little box you have put yourself into and start living life to the full extreme. Start taking chances again. It's time you veer off the beaten path in life and live a life filled with new adventures. Many times I had found myself living a life that was made up of the same old dull routine day in and day out. I then decided that this not how anyone should live life, nor is it how God intended for me to live mine. We are all intended to live the best life possible. What does that mean to live the best life possible? Does it imply that we are only to live within our means? Absolutely not! We all have the ability to live the most remarkable lives if we just allow ourselves to do it. What is stopping you? The answer is more than likely – you.

I decided a while back that I was going to start doing all the things I said I was never going to get the chance to do in my lifetime. No matter how small or even ridiculous it had seemed to me, I decided that I was going to do it all. I did this because I finally realized that God only gives us one shot at this life, and we need to take full advantage of it. I have now started to do those things. I am traveling more often and making plans to travel even more. I am getting involved in more social functions; and, more importantly, it makes me feel good (to be involved) about myself. Isn't that what life is all about? What are some of the things you have been putting on the back burner in your life? Now is the time to start moving them to the forefront.

I get so tired of people telling me that they cannot do something because of this or that. Once people tell themselves they can't, they have already defeated whatever it is they wanted to do. Stop saying that, and start doing it! I am going to share an intimate detail with you. Many of you may have noticed that I am not the most physically fit person. Heck I'll say it – I'm fat. However, I am trying to lose those pounds, but in the meantime I did something that I have always wanted to do, and it was life affirming. I went to a clothing optional beach. The key word in that sentence is "optional". It was in no way for sexual reasons, but I have always wanted to go to one.

Now planning to go was one thing, but actually being there was another. I wasn't sure how I would feel about taking my clothes off in front of others and being overweight. The key for me was that I looked around and noticed that not everybody there had a perfect body. Then in one quick motion I was standing on the beach wearing nothing. I wasn't fearful of people looking at me by any means, and nobody cared about how I looked. They were all there for the same reason that I was – to feel free. In fact, I met a few people and had quite good conversations with them. One person, an older lady, came over to me and said, "I assume this is your first time at a beach like this." I was quick to justify that it was. She gave me a piece of advice that I will take with me wherever I go. She said, "We all felt the same way the very first time." She was right. I am sure everybody was a little nervous the first time they did this. Then I thought how true that was about so many other things in life.

I took to heart what she said, and I placed my towel down on the sand and sat back for some good sun time. Unfortunately,

I am fair skinned, and with that came sunburn. Needless to say, I was sunburned pretty much everywhere. I know the next time (and there will be a next time) I am going to bring sunscreen with a higher SPF! Now I can check that off of my list of things to do. Now I know this was extreme compared to a lot of the other things that I want to do, but it is something that I have always sought to do, and now I have done it. The human body is nothing to be ashamed of. We are only that way because we believe what advertisers tell us. We believe that we have to be "society perfect" in every aspect of our bodies to be seen all natural. Untrue, we are perfect, just the way God created us. Things don't have to be perfect, to be perfect.

I want you to do me a favor. The next time you go to a mall, just look at the people that are around you. How many of them are perfect by society's standards? We all have flaws, and that is what makes us beautiful individuals. Flaws are good, and it is the flaws that make us who we are. It's funny when I tell people that I went to a clothing optional beach and shed my inhibitions; they are usually quite surprised. Yet most of them understand why I did it. People know I am a free spirit. You need to do the same thing in your life. I am not saying you need to go to a clothing optional beach, but you need to break out of your shell and start to live your life as a free spirit. Stop talking about doing things and start doing them. Don't worry about what other people think! Live your life!

Start to accomplish all the things you told yourself you were going to do, but never got around to doing. Know that you can succeed even before you begin. If little obstacles get in your way, then kick them to the curb. Remember that God does not do failure. Start small if you choose, but start. I have a lot of things I want to do on my list. The beach thing was probably the most dramatic, but I did it, and I can say with pride that I feel good about it. I am not ashamed of who I am. Also, when I shed my inhibitions at the clothing optional beach, I was not looking for anyone's approval but my own. I did talk to God and about it, and I felt that He was fine with my choice since that is how He (the universe) created us in the first place. My next task is I want to get three tattoos. I already picked them out so I know what I want. I love my body, and I am jut adding to its beauty. Just like a person may get pierced ears, I am doing the same.

I think we take things way to seriously when it comes to life. I see and talk to so many people every day who seem to be so stressed out by life and I ask why. Relieve the stress by living your life the way you desire to live. Be who YOU want to be and not who others say you should be. If you want a tattoo, then get a tattoo; if you want to wear contacts to change your eye color or dye your hair, then do it. Stop trying to conform to what society says you are supposed to be. Conforming goes against all universal plans for your life. You can't live your own life if you are trying to conform to what others say your life should be. Life is a gift, open it up and take full advantage of it by living every moment of it on your terms.

God created dreams so you could
see your potential

GUILTY PLEASURES

_____

_____

On the above lines I want you to do something for you. I want you to write down the one thing you have always desired to do in life, but you have always stopped yourself from doing it. FYI: It doesn't matter what it is. It could be anything – skydiving, painting, making more money, etc. Just take a moment and write down that one thing. We are going to ask God (the universe) to help you achieve whatever it is you put on that line.

I bet you are nervous to write down what you really desire knowing you are asking God to help you achieve it. Here is the thing…God, the universe, already knows all your wants and desires. He knows your thoughts. He already knows what you are thinking so you might as well put it down. Good, now I want you to list a few things that it will take to actually accomplish this goal. Do it on the lines below.

_____

_____

_____

Now you have your goal written down, and you have also written what it will take to make this goal a reality. How hard do you think it will be? Will it be very hard, somewhat hard, or will it be easy. The answer is up to you. It is only hard if you make it hard. In life we tend to complicate things when they do not need to be complicated. Whatever you wrote also has to be realistic. I would not recommend writing things down like you want to walk on the moon tomorrow night, because you know the possibility of that happening is quite slim. Eventually maybe you will be able to do that, but by tomorrow night is kind of pushing it. Hopefully you wrote something down that is obtainable within a justifiable timeframe. If you did, let's get started on reaching that goal.

Whatever you wrote down, I would consider it to be a guilty pleasure because it is more than likely something you want just for yourself. It should be something that once achieved, will trigger a sense of accomplishment within you. This is a guilty pleasure. It's okay to have them because we all do. Some of my guilty pleasures in life are getting the car I want to helping others who have no idea it was I who helped them (I love doing that). Whatever it is, let's work toward that goal.

Now in some people's minds this goal may feel unobtainable. It may seem as if there is no chance you will ever achieve your goal, but the first thing you need to know is that this objective IS achievable. It is possible. You need to tell yourself continuously that it is possible, but even more crucial is that you need to believe it. You can do anything you set your mind to. Conquering that part is half the battle. First things first – take a deep breath and let it out slowly. Take another deep breath and let it out slowly again, and then do it again one more time. Now focus on what it will take to accomplish this goal.

The three main points to achieving any goal are the following:

- You need to *know* that you will achieve it.
- You need to *focus* on it.
- You need to *act* upon it.

"Know, focus, and act" are the three key elements to making any goal a reality. Once you "know', you need to move on to "focus". Make this goal a passion of yours. Make it part of your everyday life. Once you do that you need to "act" upon it. Remember sitting back and doing nothing accomplishes nothing. Therefore it you don't act, you will never accomplish it. Do not let fear get in the way. I remember when I was younger and first started dating. When asking someone out, I hated to a get a "no" because I always felt rejected. I would get a couple of "no's" of out the way, and then I was done for the night. On the other hand my friend would get a no and then move on to the next person. He said he was working under something called the law of averages. What the heck was that? He said that the more "no's" he got, the better. He said eventually someone would say yes, and you know what – he was right. He would keep going, and the next thing you know he was out on the dance floor having a good time while I sat and sulked at the bar.

Wow, have times changed for me. Now I accept rejection as a compliment, because I know that the yes is out there, just like you with your goal. You will find the yes; you just need to keep going through all the rejections to find it – the yes. Think of it like this: the more "no's" you get, the better because you are just getting them out of the way. As you continue to pursue your goal, the actuality of it coming to fruition becomes even greater with each rejection. You can't let simple things like a "no" get in the way of you achieving success. As an example, think about all the rejection Thomas Edison came upon, but He reached his goal of creating the lightbulb, among many other things. Never be disappointed by a no in life; in fact, let it get you excited for all the possibilities that are now ready to come to realization.

Some people struggle day to day because they choose to live like that. I know I did at one time. However, I now choose to move on with my life and continue to live each day to its fullest. I set goals every day, and when I reach them I set new ones. I don't always hit my goal each day, but I also don't let that stop me from eventually achieving them. I know if I work hard towards them they will eventually come to be, and then I can smile and move on the next one. You need to do the same. You need to know that any goal you set is obtainable, and you will reach it if you just don't give up. Also, if you leave any of the three keys out (knowing, focusing and acting), you make it more difficult to fulfill your goals, not impossible, just more difficult. It is just a matter of you knowing that it will happen. Remember these words when you are reaching for your goals: give up and get nothing; keep trying and get everything. The choice is yours my friend.

If you simply live to impress others
then you will never truly live.

3, 2, 1 ... LIFT OFF

Right now God (the universe) is giving you the opportunity to do something extraordinary in your life. He is giving you the chance to re-launch it. It is time to take a stance and to start believing in you. I personally believe that you only need two things to succeed at anything in life. The first is to believe in God the universe and yourself, and the second is to have faith in both. I truly believe that. It all starts with a belief that anything is possible, and the faith that it is achievable. When people ask me about my belief in God, a God that I know I cannot see, I tell them this: "I can't see the wind, but I know it is there. I can't see my brain, but I know it's there." I know in my heart that God does exist. I can feel Him in my soul. When I talk with Him I can sense His presence in the room, and I have an unwavering faith in my belief.

This is your opportunity to build on the relationship you have with God. It is your time to rewrite what you have started. It's kind of like writing a book and then making changes as you go along. Thus for this experiment I want you to write down where you thought you would be at in life at this very moment in time. Take out a piece of paper and start writing. Maybe you thought you would be married right now. Maybe you thought you would be the president of a large corporation. Or maybe you thought you would own your own little bakery somewhere. Wherever you thought you would be, write that down.

Okay, do you have it written down? If so, take that piece of paper with both hands and fold it in half. Then fold it in half one more time, and then one more time for the fun of it. Now here is the important part…throw it away. What? Throw it away? Yes, because you are right where you are supposed to be in life. Maybe one day you will be wherever it is that you wrote down, but for now you are exactly where you are meant to be at this very moment in time.

Keeping that in mind, you have been given a second chance to re-launch what your own history will be. When people talk about you, will they talk about your past, or where you are going right now? The choice is yours.

Be aware that not many people realize they have second chances in life. In fact, I'll bet you did not even realize that you also have third chances, fourth chances, and fifth chances, and so on and so on.

Yes, God has given you the ability to scrap your past and to start all over again wherever and whenever you want to. In fact you can start right now if you choose. That is the key to re-launching your life. You need to choose to do it and don't wait. Start right now!

I have seen so many people who are down on themselves because of past issues. They are called past issues for a reason, because they are in the past. No matter what that past has entailed, it is over, and it is time to move on. Let it go and move on to a new and exciting future filled with whatever you choose it to be filled with. Remember earlier when I asked you to write down a goal (hopefully you did)? Now is the time to make that goal a part of your new life. If you wish, make it the focal point.

All I ask is that you find something and work towards it. If you fall off kilter, start over. You are re-launching your future, and only you can choose what your future will hold. You have total control over your own destiny. God will be more than happy to help guide you to where you need to be – you just need to start. Confucius said, "A journey of a thousand miles begins with a single step." It is time to take that step.

Hmm, maybe starting is your problem. Maybe you don't know how to get things going. Well, how is your relationship with God the universe doing? Is it strong? Do you include Him in all aspects of your life? If so, then He is ready and willing to help you achieve whatever it is you want to achieve. In my last book I talked a lot about God moments. The moments where God stepped into my life and guided me to where it was that I needed to be. Sometimes I had to let go and let Him guide the ship for a while. It is okay to ask God for assistance. In fact, He wants you to ask for assistance. God the universe loves you so much that he only wants to see you succeed. You cannot spell success without "U" (you). God wants to see you be happy. What will make you happy?

Let me ask you this, if you could re-launch your life right now what is the first thing you would do? Well let's make that a priority in your life. No matter what it is, let's move that to the top of the list along with the goal you wrote down. Maybe it's the same as the goal that you had already written down earlier. Whatever it is, let's get working on it. Your past is gone. The slate is clean, and you are heading in a new direction. I have a list of things I want to accomplish over the next year. I told you about the beach (which I accomplished) and the tattoos. Though they were not at the top of my list, they were something that I could easily do and mark off quickly. My current list has 12 items on it, one for each month of the year. I know by achieving each individual goal, my life is on track to do what I want with it. Although, I still give back to humanity, I am also taking care of my needs at the same time.

God the universe is so good to all of us. God is willing to wipe our slate clean just by asking Him to do so. I asked you earlier about your relationship with God. You have to be serious about that. I never start the day without thanking Him for what He has done for me, and I continue to do so throughout the day. God (the universe) is the reason I am able to do the things I want to do. I cannot change my past, but if I could, having a better relationship with God would be one thing I wish I had started earlier. I do not believe in living with any regrets, but I can only imagine where I would be right now if I had. With that said, I can't change the past and neither can you; therefore, we are right where we are supposed to be. We only have the ability to change what we can, and that is this moment and our future. We have the ability to make any changes we want at any time, so why not start now. Below list three immediate changes you are going to make in your life. Once done, make a copy and keep it with you. Remember the changes you make right now are going to be for a better future, so once again choose them wisely and go for it!

_____

_____

_____

You can't find
true love on the outside
if you can't find it
on the inside first.

YOUR GOD GIVEN BIRTHRIGHT

Repeat after me: I can do anything. Did you say it? I know you read it to yourself, but did you say it? I mean out loud in front of God and everybody? Try it again, and say it out loud: I can do anything!

Now you know that you can do anything. Just reading the words on a page does not make them possible. However, saying them out loud makes the impossible become possible. Now you have to believe it. You have to believe that you can do anything that you put your mind to. You actually have to believe that the improbable is probable. You are going to be making some incredible changes in your life for the better, but you need to believe what you tell yourself. This is an affirmation that you can do whatever it is you desire to do with your life.

I read stories all the time about people who have done extraordinary things. Things they never thought they could achieve, but somehow they managed to do them. Do you know why those people succeeded? Because they believed they could do it, and they had the faith to make it a reality. If they thought they were going to fail, then why would they keep trying? Those people keep trying because they know failure is not an option. With a solid belief in themselves and strong faith, they continue trying until they eventually accomplish whatever it was they were trying to accomplish. The simple answer to why those people succeeded is that they already knew the secret to success, and that is to already know that they would succeed.

Here it is, another key to help you when you are starting to change your life for the better – already know that you will succeed. This is one of the most important parts of change. The rest is just putting the effort into it, and making it happen; and "it" can be anything in life. Remember failure is not an option, because failure does not exist. Therefore, this makes success your only option. Ergo, no matter what you do in life, you are going to be successful. You have to already know this. Anytime you believe that you have failed, it is *not* a failure, but a learning experience. You now know what not do in that particular situation. Thus, if I told you that in life there is an option to only be successful would you believe me? By believing in that success, you are on your way to changing your life. If you do not then you need to re-read what you just read. *Success is the only option, because we do not do failure.*

I have spoken to so many people that feel their lives are failures. I can relate to them, because I used to think that way about my life. I came to God thinking that I was a disappointment to Him, and in spite of that, He convinced me that I was not a failure, but a complete success. I was doing what I was supposed to do and that was learning. If that's the truth, then I have been learning day in and day out for many years. In fact, it was too many years in my mind, but just the right amount of time in God's. You too may have felt this way or maybe you feel this way right now, and that your life has been nothing more than one big train wreck. Well here is some good news for you... God (the universe) can help you get the cars back on the track and point you in the right direction. In order to do this you need to be willing to accept the fact that you are not, nor have you ever been, a failure in your life. When I tell you that you can do anything you want to do in life, I am not just telling you that to make you feel better. I am telling you that because it is the truth. There is an old saying, "the truth will set you free", so there you are, free to be you.

Take a moment out of each day and affirm to yourself that you are a success in life. Don't forget to thank God the universe for all He has done for you either. We need to praise ourselves in the good times and the bad. Standing before you now is the most incredible life you could ever have imagined, and it is there just for the taking. Who do you need to ask? The answer is you. You hold the key to your future. It is right before you. Grasp it and live it. Keep telling yourself that you can do anything. Don't listen to those who say differently. Those are the people who try and knock down others who are living a life better than they ever will. Those people refuse to acknowledge that they hold the solution to their own problems, and that my friend will get you nowhere.

You have a God given right to be successful in everything you do. Yes, a God given right. God himself gave this right to you at your birth. It is your birthright, and you have the ability to make it possible whenever you choose to do so. If only more people knew this, just think how much better the world would be right now. It is our responsibility to share this information with them as I am sharing it with you. Spread the message of success and enjoy the fruits of your labor.

You are a success and always have been, period.

Dreams are not meant
to be chased;
they are meant to be lived.

SUDDEN AWARENESS (INSTANT LOVE)

One could simply describe sudden awareness as an unexpected knowing of something. That's how it is with God (the universe) in your life. When you start to understand your relationship with Him you have this unexpected knowing that a power greater than yours is now around you. It's a feeling like no other that you have ever felt before. The best way I can describe this to you is a sensation of instant love. It feels like an immediate release of all the stress in your life and feeling that everything is great. It can sometimes send your emotions into overload, which I can attest to. My emotions, which were once more straight laced, have now become more present. It is like I can feel the pain of others; I feel their sorrow, and I feel their joy. I am definitely more emotional now than I was before, but it is a good emotional.

This is what you can expect when you start to understand your connection to God. God is faithful to all, and expects nothing less from them. It is a mutual admiration for each other. As your love grows, so does His. God the universe has given you a remarkable gift: the gift of sudden awareness – the gift to feel universal love towards others. With this gift you can feel the intense emotions that others are feeling. You can relate to them on a higher level than you ever have before. Once that gift is realized, and the universal bond is strong, you will notice things a little differently. Let me explain.

There have been numerous times when I have walked up to a complete stranger and knew what was going on in his or her life. The stranger would ask me how I knew, and my response was (and always is), "God told me." I have met numerous people who have done the same thing. It does not happen all the time, but it does happen. This is due to the understanding we have built between us and God the universe.

Once that understanding is built, you will feel as if you are one with all. It is automatic. God will be there in all the areas of your life. You will find that it always seems as if you are in the right place at the right time. This is God connecting with you and guiding you to help others. If you want God the universe to help you, then it is only fair that you return this gift. You do this by continually living the life you have envisioned for yourself and by helping others along the way.

Live life to its fullest, and you will become more aware of your ability to succeed. You will see your life as God sees your life – filled with achievements, precision, excellence, fulfillment, aptness, and the realization that you can be whoever you desire to be by just knowing. It is time to make the decision to know who and what you are; it is perfection in the eyes of God.

The beauty of the wind can be seen in the dance of the leaves.

SPIRITUAL KARMA
(The spiritual law of cause and effect)

What is Spiritual Karma? Spiritual Karma pertains to your Soul. It is the aura (energy) you put out into the world. It is your soul's outlook on your destiny. It is who and what you are. We all have it, but not all of us are in touch with it. I want to reiterate once again that you are exactly where you are supposed to be in life. No matter what situation you are in, you are right where you are supposed to be. Why, because you have put yourself there, by way of spiritual karma.

I know that may sound confusing, because if you are in a negative place in life you may feel there is no way you would ever put yourself in that situation. The truth of the matter is this: every decision you have ever made in life has brought you to the place you are at right now. I have been in some very bad situations because I put myself there. Whether you are having financial difficulties or relationship problems, you are there because you have chose to put yourself there. I know this sounds harsh, but it is the truth. However, there is good news. Since you put yourself there, you can also take yourself out of that position. You have the power to do it and you can begin right now!

So, what do you need to do to change your Spiritual Karma? The first thing is to understand that you need to change. The second thing is to change your attitude to the positive. I know how hard it is to try and be positive when the entire world feels like it is falling in on you. You must know that you have the power to be positive. It is within your soul. Your soul is so powerful that it can override all the negative energy. It can bring you back to the path of enlightenment. Enlightenment is to live in the spiritual realm of life; to be one with your spiritual side and more importantly, to be one with all that God has created. This is very powerful. You need to realize that you have this gift of power.

Now, how do you get in touch with that part of your life? In plain words, you need to connect with your soul. God has given you this amazing gift. Your soul is the epicenter of who you are. We all have a soul, but very few of us ever get in contact with it. The best way (I find) to do this is through meditation. Meditation is your ability to get in contact with your inner-self. This is best explained by saying that praying is one way we communicate with God the universe and meditation is how we receive the answers.

To connect with your soul is to finally know your true self. I believe that I have a direct connection with God through prayer and meditation just as you do. This is a gift from God. Needless to say, to change your life and to start living in a positive mindset, you should start to meditate. Yes, I also believe in the power of prayer. Prayer is just another way to communicate with God. Communication is the key. I have been through many challenges in the last few years, and because of this gift from God, I have been able to change my entire outlook on things. I have changed my Spiritual Karma and my own destiny. You also have the ability to choose your own destiny and where you choose to go, it is up to you, the choice is yours.

If you want to be in sync with your life, then you need to change your Spiritual Karma to get there. You can change your entire life within a matter of moments. Take some time today and seek out the knowledge of becoming one with your soul. Remember that you choose your own path, so choose wisely. We are all on a journey of self-discovery, but where your journey will take you is in your hands.

Don't let the pain of your past
dictate the pleasure
of this moment!

Complaining about problems

How many of you complain about your life? Go ahead you can admit it. I will. I used to complain about my life all the time. Whether it was work, money or a relationship - I was always complaining about something. You know where that got me in life? Nowhere. This is what I say about complaining: you cannot complain about things if you are not willing to do something about it.

I would just sit there and expect things to change. The problem with that is the situations usually got even worse. What I learned from those experiences is that I had to get involved in my own life. I had to become an active participant in every aspect of it. No more sitting on the sidelines. I had to get in the game. I had to make some necessary changes.

The first thing I did was I sat down and made a list of my problems and then I prioritized them. Sometimes the problems I was complaining about were a lot bigger in my mind, but didn't seem so big once I put them on paper and looked at them. I also found out by doing this that the solutions seemed to come easier. I would literally work out my problems on paper first. By doing so, I added a very important part to the problem-solving equation. I added the aspect of visualization. I got to see the answers in front of me and in my mind that made the solutions that much more possible.

The next time you are complaining about a problem try writing it down and working out the solution on paper. You just might find the answers you were looking for right before your eyes.

If life is difficult,

it's only because we choose it to be that way.

THE THREE R'S
Relax, Release, and Revive

I know sometimes life can be a little troublesome. Heck, it can be downright nasty, but the point I am trying to make is that you need to relax during these situations. Release the negatives and revive yourself. Stressing out will only make whatever the situation is much more difficult for you to handle.

In life, it is so easy for us to take the low road, but on your journey of discovering your true self, it is important to maintain a level of consistency with all that is around you. An exercise I like to do is to listen to some calming meditation music and bring myself back to a point of serenity. It is in these times that I find I can think more clearly and the problems before me seem to be less insurmountable as I once imagined. I also like to do breathing exercises to release the negatives and breathe in the positives. I realized a few years ago that most of my problems were merely thoughts I was manifesting. Change my thoughts, and I change my outcome.

You see your imagination is a key that can unlock anything within you. You can make your mind imagine anything, whether it is good or bad. With your imagination, you can take what most would see as a very minor problem and turn it into one that seems like the world is caving in on you. If you are going to use this gift of imagination, it is best used as a positive in your life.

Okay, time for another exercise. I want you to find a place wherever you are at this very moment and think of a situation that you need to take care of. Then I want you to take a deep breath and meditate for a few minutes. Then I want you to come back to whatever the situation was and come up with a solution. The answer is there inside of you. Imagine all the scenarios that will help you take care of whatever it is you need to take care of. Imagine that it is done. What was the solution? I have had some very troubling periods in my life, but it was not until I focused on solving them that they actually went away.

Meditation is all about focusing on your inner self or your inner calm, if you will. When you meditate do not meditate only on the façade (outside). Meditate by ascending to that place of pure thought and wisdom deep within you. Focus on all that is before you. Reflect on all that is you and see the big picture of life. I know I talked about some of this earlier, but now it is time to work on all the things that you need to get done to eventually get you to the place you were destined to be. Your future is in your hands. What are you doing about it?

I am merely here to help guide you to understanding your true infinite potential. It is through this understanding that I am fulfilling my own purpose in life, or humanity if you will. You must remove any and all blockages that stop you from achieving success. I know nobody likes to face their problems head on, but it is so important that you do this to solve them quickly. It is like facing an enemy. You can confront them, but in the end one must find the way to defeat them or they will continue to bring negatives into your life.

As a result, here are ten focus points to relaxing, releasing and reviving yourself by removing stress and problems from your everyday life. First, you must take a deep breath and release. Secondly, relax and stay calm. Third, begin to meditate. Fourth, focus on all the answers that are before you. Fifth, you need to understand that all the solutions for any situation are within you. Sixth, you must trust in God and yourself. Seventh, you must know the final answer will come to realization. Eighth, you must apply the solution. Ninth, you must not stop. Tenth, you must believe that everything is going to be fine no matter how things look on the outside.

Remember you are a part of God. Do you really think God the universe would not place within you the answers that one would need to be happy? Of course He would and He did. As human beings we just need to find answers to the questions that are before us. They are there, and now is the time to find them. Just remember to relax, release, and revive yourself.

To be only satisfied with your life
is to say that you
have not really lived yet.

IS "OKAY" REALLY OKAY
(The power of words)

When you think of the word "okay," what do you think of? I think of the term "just settling." The reason I say this is simple. For example, "okay" is the word I tell the wait staff at a restaurant when they ask about food and I think it's not good or bad; it's just average. "Okay" is just average, and in this life we need to strive to be above average. If you are permitting yourself to live an "average" life, then I think you need to start making some changes, and start living an above average life. Doing so will not only help you, but it will also show others in tough situations that it can be done. You have now become a conveyor of your own spiritual message.

Therefore, what do people do to live an above average existence? They do what you are doing right this very moment. People are always striving to be better off than they were just a moment ago. They know the true power of what being average is, and they don't like it. Awakened people understand that they need to change things like the words they use, in order to change the eventual outcome of any situation.

You have to come to the realization that just being mediocre is not going to get you anywhere. If you don't, you will just be spinning your tires and going nowhere. Understand that language is a large part of moving ahead (to stop those tires from just spinning). Understand that eventually if you don't change how you see your life, you will become stuck in the rut of just getting by, and that is no way to live your life.

When talking about your life (or when people ask) try and stay away from these type of words if at all possible: *standard, normal, regular, typical, ordinary, mediocre, common, and usual* to name a few.

Instead you want to use words like these: *grand, breathtaking, tremendous, amazing, awe inspiring, astounding, brilliant, remarkable, awesome, terrific, fantastic, wonderful, stunning, astonishing, and incredible* to name a few.

When you use positive words to describe yourself it makes you feel better. It makes you feel like you have a strong sense of accomplishment (and you do). You need to see that words are very powerful and your choice and usage of them can make or break any dream that you may be focusing on right this very moment. Therefore, starting right now it is imperative to choose your words wisely and to use them at the same time. Words can cause the mind and body to feel pleasure or pain. Which would you rather feel? In fact, don't even answer that question, because you already know the answer to it. The answer is obviously pleasure. Stop using words that cause pain and use the ones that are gratifying, but not just for you, but for everyone around you, trust me they are listening.

To see God, one must only look within one's own self.

LOST? FOLLOW YOUR G.P.S.

Not sure what to do next? Don't worry because your inner G.P.S. will help guide you. G.P.S. (in this case) stands for God's Perfect System. Yes, God is helping you to reach all of your dreams through your soul. He is working day and night to see that everything is perfectly aligned just for you. How does that happen? It happens by building and maintaining your connection with God the universe.

Today of all days you need to know how important it is to include God in all you do. He wants to be a part of your life. He is the reason you are here. You need to know how important this connection is. I've seen far to many people stray from God, and in return their spiritual life falls apart. The next thing you know the domino effect begins. How do I know? I was one of those people who strayed and experienced it first-hand. My life was in shambles before I realized what the problem was. The problem was that I wasn't including God in everything I do. Today I always include Him. I never start the day without talking to Him, and I make it a point to end my day the same way. Everything that is happening in my life is because of my connection with God, including writing this book.

Yes, I can tell you countless stories about all the great things that God is doing in my life, but I feel the need to stress to you the importance of what He is doing in your life. If you are not reaping all the benefits of being a creation of God, then I suggest you take a good look at the connection you have built with Him.

When you were born, God the universe put you on the path to your destiny. Like most others, with the gift of freewill you may tend to stray from the path and create your own false destiny. Creating your own destiny can be pleasing to God the universe. However, it can be displeasing when you take the path that is filled with heartache and pain.

Over the years I have spoken with drug addicts, gamblers, prostitutes, alcoholics, etc. Most of these people had two things in common. First, they had taken God out of the equation and second, they wanted to change, but did not know how to do it. Nobody grows up thinking "I want to be a drug addict." God's Perfect System entails just what it says: it is perfect. It is a guide for you to follow on your travels throughout your life. The power to do so is within you. It is in your soul.

We all have to make choices in life. Sometimes we make good choices and sometimes we make not so good choices. Yet in either event, we make choices. We all try to follow what we think is best for our lives. However, this had gotten me into a lot of trouble over the years. Once I realized the importance of my connection with God the universe, my life changed. I understood that I create my own path to follow and through guidance (prayer and meditation) anything is possible.

God is ready and willing to help you achieve all of your dreams if you would just let him. Open the door to happiness and let God the universe in, and tomorrow will be a brand-new day filled with many blessings. Turn on your G.P.S. and see it for yourself.

The past to your destiny is not always meant to be easy.

It is meant to be fulfilling.

COUNTING CHICKENS

I always wondered about the saying, "Don't count your chickens before they hatch". I guess the reason behind it is in case some hatchlings don't make it. However, I want you to count your chickens before they hatch! This goes back to knowing what you have before you had it. Whatever you choose to do in life, know that you are already going to be successful at it.

When I talked about my book (the one you are now reading) I told everybody how successful it was. They usually looked at me oddly because I was still in the process of writing it. I would tell them that I could already see what this book will bring into my life and the lives of many others. I knew exactly how it would be received. People need to understand that in life, you can't just sit there and watch the world go by. You need to grab on with both hands and take the ride. Envision your destiny. Connect with your soul and plan what you are going to do with your life. In my mind I knew this book would be very successful. You're reading it right? Therefore, this book must be a success!

Success is not something that is inherited or learned it is something that was instilled in all of us at birth. Sometimes, it just takes some of us a little longer to understand that. I want you to do something again. On the following line I want you to write down the type of vehicle you are going to own. Not the vehicle you want or the car you need, but the one you always think about and dream of.

_____

_____

_____

Did you choose something exotic like a Porsche or a Ferrari? Or did you pick something like a mini-van or pick-up truck? In either case, you picked the car that you are going to own. Now, you have to know it. You need to envision it. You need to see yourself sitting behind the steering wheel and actually driving it. You need to feel your hands truly gripping that steering wheel and taking a deep breath of that new car smell. Do you see it? Can you feel it? Can you smell it? If so, then you need to keep that feeling going. Take it with you wherever you go. Very soon that vehicle will be yours. I keep a picture of my Corvette convertible in my wallet. It's red with a black top and beige interior. I can see it. I know one day it will be mine. Why? Because I already know it.

It does not matter what you do in life. You just need to understand that no matter what you are striving for, you will be very successful at it. I remember a few year ago, I always talked about being broke and losing everything. Needless to say, because I envisioned it so much, I became successful at it. I was successfully bankrupt! Do you know how much effort and energy it takes to lose everything over the span of a year and a half? It takes a lot. Imagine if I had put all that energy into already knowing that I would be financially successful. Where would I be today? The answer is right where I am, because we are where we are supposed to be. If you are broke and tired of it, then do something about it. Your destiny requires you to do something. Today you may be broke, but tomorrow you may be…who knows. You know! Start counting those chickens today!

In life we always have two choices.

One is to do something, and the second is to do nothing.

Either choice will get you to the destination you are currently creating.

MIND SOUL CONNECTION
(MSC)

There is a fine line between the natural world and the spiritual world. Unknowingly you travel in and out of both realms on a daily basis. You have the ability to actually be in two places at once. How exciting is that? Therefore, if anyone asks you how a person can be in two places at once, now you will have an answer for them.

To live within the spiritual realm, you must first know that this side of you exists. Obviously, you know the physical realm exists since you are in it right now reading this book. It is when you put this book down and start to apply the logic from it that you are transported into the spiritual side. Your spiritual side is filled with all that can be and all that ever was. It is the largest database of you. It holds more information than one can ever experience in a lifetime, or does it?

Getting in touch with this side of your life is very significant. What your destiny holds is within this section of your life. Many people who have discovered this side have gone on to do great things. Though people may say that they are spiritual, the truth of the matter is that if they have not touched that element of their inner being, then they are not. No one can claim to be spiritual unless they have been able to find that deep down point within themselves where everything that was, is. "Was" is the past tense, and you can recall anything into the present tense once you are able to connect with this part of you.

So how does one get to this connection with their spirituality? You must become solitary with your own soul. You must reach down to the very core of your being and start to connect with all that is and will ever be. Your spiritual side is filled with all the joy that one could ever imagine, but it also holds the key to whatever it is that you will become. You become what you think about, and what you think about starts in the soul and travels to the mind. There you will find all the thoughts that you have ever created. Between you and your soul is all that ever was or now is.

In your mind things like inspiration, theories, philosophies, concepts, notions, ideas, beliefs, and opinions are formed. They are formed from your independent thought. That which was once nothing, becomes that which now is. This is based on the principles of the mind soul connection (MSC). This connection can only be achieved through your own unconstrained reflection within yourself. You must first ease the constraints of your own consciousness in order to find what is hidden within this relationship of the mind and soul. Here you can find what is known as enlightenment. This gives all of us the experience of what is known as clarity. Thus you are able to know your true self.

You must remain cognizant of what is around you at all times. Your mind and soul are on a continual basis of communication with each other. Once you have found that line of the mind and soul connection (MSC), you must continue to seek out more information from it. Within it you will be able to move forward with your ability to recognize your very being as an energy source that continually vibrates creating who you are in the physical world. Everything you see is energy, and everything you see is created by the beginning of that which now is. This is the origin of all. This is the beginning of that which now is. This is the beginning of you. All that God the universe has created has been designed from energy. You are energy or power.

From this power (energy) all that ever will be is formed. That is why I talk a lot about you being a part of creation itself. As a part of God the Universe you are a spiritual being that has the ability to seek out its own source of existence.

You have the direct line to the creator of all that is and ever will be – the Alpha and Omega. You, my friend, are a part of the very foundation of creation. To be able to know this and to connect with it is very powerful. This is why you are able to be or do whatever it is you choose. You have the ability to be anything, because you have the energy (power) to do so. Once you find this connection, life, as you know it, will never be the same. Thoughts will become more lucid and you will become much more aware of your transparency as a being. As a result of this you will now become part of what is called oneness- the ability to become one with all that is and ever was.

I know this may seem kind of deep for some to understand, but know that as you start to connect with your inner being, all of this will become second nature to you. Your mind soul connection (MSC) will become stronger as you become more connected with who you are spiritually. You will become more in-tune with everything around you. Thoughts will now become reality. You will also be able to understand all the wisdom that your soul possesses. This will give you the capability to use this gift more intelligently in your decision-making. You will now be one with your soul, thus making you one with God.

You are exactly at the point in life where you have put yourself.

Don't like it? Change it!

FLIP THAT SWITCH

Alter, modify, vary, transform, revolutionize, amend, modify, adjust, exchange, replace, swap, switch, convert and change. What do all these words have in common? They are all things you need to do to live the life you desire. You need to do all these things. Do me a favor (again). Below write down one thing you would like to change about yourself right now.

_____

_____

_____

Now this is what you need to work on. You have set another goal for yourself. The change you choose to make can be anything you desire it to be. You need to concentrate on making this a reality though. Remember, you are a part of Generation You. As a part of this generation, your thoughts become realities. Therefore, you need to stay focused on achieving whatever it is you wrote down about yourself. Let me let you in on a little secret. I did the same thing, and I wrote down that I wanted to lose weight and I have. Mostly for health purposes, because I am fine with my body as it is (was). You need to flip that switch inside of you that will put this goal into motion.

Let's face it – almost everybody has something about them they would like to change. Whether it is their body image or the way they see the world, everyone has something (they want to change). The solution to making a change is to just do it. Procrastination is the death of change. I can say that when it comes to procrastinating, I did my fair share. Most changes are done to make people feel good about who they are. If this is your reason, then why wait? Start today and make that change. I know for me that losing weight will not happen overnight, but it will happen, because I have the faith that it will. The same goes for you. Whatever change(s) you are looking to make right now, know that it might not happen overnight, but it will happen once you put your plan of how to do it into action.

If I was to open up my bag of procrastination, I bet I would find thousands of things I intended to do, but just never got around to them, like losing weight. I have always wanted to lose weight, but I would always start diets and then never finish them. Or I would never start them at all. I was (the key word was) addicted to food. It was my drug of choice. No matter what was going on in life, I turned to food. In fact after my divorce, I gained an extra hundred pounds over the next year. It happened over such a long period of time, that I never really noticed. Then one day I took a good look at myself in the mirror and knew I had to change. However, let me say that I am fine with my body and the way it looks. I am losing weight to become healthier. (Plus, if I was to somehow get a set of six pack abs, I can live with that.)

The point I am trying to make is that we all need to start now if we are going to make any changes to improve our lives. Don't keep putting things off until tomorrow. Do them today. Remember, we are not guaranteed a tomorrow, so we need to live every moment we are given. No more postponing, dragging your feet, delaying, deferring, dawdling or putting off. As I always say, the time to act is now. Remember to flip that switch and get going. A better you awaits.

In life we tend to see the hard problems and the not simple solutions — that is human nature.

ARE YOU PREPARED

There is an old story about two houses that was written long ago. One was built on a solid rock and the other built on sand. Although both builders built their homes with pride and thought they would last, only one survived a storm. Obviously the one that survived was the one built on the solid rock, but this is a great perspective on life in general. How are you prepared to handle any storms in your life?

Over the years I have found that the easiest way to achieving your dreams, and weathering the storms, is to get ready for them to become realities. This way you are prepared when they do come to fruition. Take for example, the car I know I am going to have soon. I have already prepared myself mentally to receive it. I have even gone as far as to know where in the garage I will park it and what will be next to it. Oh, by the way, did I mention that I have not purchased the house yet, but I can already see that too.

When deciding that you are going to make some changes in your life, you need to start organizing what is around you, mentally, physically, and spiritually to receive those changes. You need to be ready in all three areas of your life. Sometimes the smallest things have the biggest impacts, so are you ready in all three areas? I remember when I kissed a girl for the first time. I was in first grade, and we kissed in the window well during recess. Looking back, it was no big deal, but back then it was like winning the lottery. I won't mention her name, but later that year she moved, and I was heartbroken. To this day I have no idea where she is, but I will always remember that first kiss. What does this have to do with making changes? It has everything to do with it because (even as a first grader) I prepared for that kiss (storm); I wore my best clothes to school, combed my hair, and I was ready for that kiss.

See even as kids we know to prepare for changes in our life. Did that one moment change my life? Of course it did. I wanted more kisses! It put me on the path to eventually dating and so forth. As we grow older we start to forget that. We forget to be prepared. We forget to expect the unexpected. We forget to expect the expected – like our dreams becoming realities. There is another old saying that says, "If you can believe it, you can achieve it". Do you believe that? Sure you do, because that's what belief is all about. It's about already knowing that your dreams are going to come to fulfillment. It's that moment of anticipation that keeps you motivated. We need to keep that going in order to realize all that we could ever have imagined. We need to prepare for the storms in life. The storm is coming. Are you ready? What is your house built on? Rock or sand? Again, the choice is yours.

If you forget about humanity,
then theoretically you
are forgetting about yourself.

START LIVING OR START . . .

I am sure you have heard the saying "start living or start dying". Well that is pretty much the truth when it comes to life. You need to start living or start dying – it's your choice. As you age the body begins to breakdown. However, due to medical advances you are able to stay healthier and live longer. This gives us even more time to enjoy the fruits of our labor. Sitting here typing I think back to the days when I would just sit around and do nothing all day long. Just kick back and relax. What's the point of doing nothing all day long? Relaxation is fine sometimes, but not all the time. You need to enjoy life to its fullest. You need to get out and do some things.

Here we go again, I want you to make another list, but this time I want you to list about ten things that you want to do. Maybe you want to travel? Maybe you want to ride a roller coaster for the first time? Maybe you just want to have an exciting day at the beach playing volleyball? Whatever it is, write it down below.

_____

_____

_____

_____

_____

_____

_____

Did you write them down? If you don't have ten things written down, you can always add to the list later. Now look at your list. If you could choose anyone of them, which one would you like to do first? Did you pick one? Great, now do it! Whatever it is, just do it! I know it sounds easier said than done, but there is a way to accomplish whatever it is you wish to accomplish. If it is important to you, you will find a way. Do not become full of excuses. Work towards making whatever it is you desire to do a reality. Remember once you say you can't, you are right, and it ends there.

I was talking to somebody recently about living life on "your" terms. Doing what you desire to do and enjoying life to its fullest. The person I was talking to believes that he should be doing ministry work. That person has a full time job working ridiculous hours for not much money. This person believes that he has a higher calling in life and he is right. Now my friend just needs to make the decision to do what he knows is right for him. I know in my heart he will make the best decision for his life, but it has to be his choice.

The same goes for you. Where are you at in life? This is a simple question, but usually followed by a not so simple answer. People always tell me that they would like to do this or that, but they have kids or their job gets in the way. Those are excuses. There is always a way. If you really wanted to live your life on your terms then there is a way. Others have done it! Whatever that way is, you must find it. Remember, to help get you started you need to already know that whatever it is you want to do will happen (knowing over wanting). The life you know you will live is right before you. It is there for the asking, so ask for it and know you will receive it.

The power of belief is resilient to all that is around it. It is always there when you need it and never goes away. Subsequently, if you truly believe that everything you want to achieve is possible, then it is. Don't close the doors God is opening for you. Do you know who has the most influence over your life? The answer is you, but you also have the power to give all or some of that control away. You do this by giving your control away to all the negatives in your life. DO NOT DO THIS! DO NOT LET THIS HAPPEN! Take control of your life, and be the person who will not let anything stand in your way. Be the person who succeeds in life because you already know you will. Be the person who is reaching his or her dreams because you understand that the world is yours. Be the person who lived life everyday like he or she was dying. That is the person who in the end can look back and smile knowing he or she was victorious in living life on his or her terms.

Always lead, live, and love from your soul.

You Have the Lead

While I was writing this book I had someone ask me if I thought people would believe the things I am telling them. I thought for a second, and I told him that I wasn't asking people to believe in me as much as they should believe in themselves and their own personal experiences. What you are reading are mostly my experiences from God the universe, and you will have your own. However, I have noticed since talking to people that "wow" moment when they realize that they have experienced similar moments in their own lives, but never realized the connection.

That's what this is all about. It's about experiencing life to its fullest and learning new and exciting ways to encounter all it has to offer. Life is too short not to experience as much of it as we can. We are all on our own journey in life, and we need to be able to encompass it for all it is worth. Do you agree? With that said, trust me when I say that you will have your own experiences. I know in the greater scheme of things life is not supposed to be all about you, but you need to make "you" a main focal point in order to fulfill your own destiny.

My experience with all of this has changed my life to such a degree that I can imagine all that lies ahead. I am excited about all the possibilities that I awake to on a daily basis. I have a better (more honest) relationship with people, and I experience things on an entirely new plateau. I don't feel sorry for anyone who is not where I am at spiritually, because I know that they can be at the same point whenever they choose to do so. As I share this information with you, I hope you are sharing it with others as well. It is important that you share your experiences, because someone who needs to hear it is waiting to. People don't know about our experiences unless we open up and talk about them (or write books in some cases).

Because of your connection to God the universe, you play a very pivotal role in life. You play the role of... you. Yes, you play you, and your roll is a very significant part of what God has created. Understand that you are the only one that was chosen to play your part. Then, I guess you can say you were typecast. This is how important your life is to this world. It is critical that you realize the importance of your existence (roll). Understand that you play a very large part, but in the beginning, we only play a supporting role until we come to the understanding of who and what we are. These are the same rolls that others around the world play, and together all of us make up the cast of Humanity. Does this help you grasp how important you are in the eyes of God? This is why God the universe wants you to live the best life possible. He wants to move you from a supporting role to a lead role, and only you can do that. You have the power to do it. Now is the time to use this power! You are the star of your life, so now smile for the cameras and... ready, set, action...

Don't live your life in chapters,
live in moments

(there are so many more of them).

Stepping Stones

It is so easy to fall back to where you once were after starting to make changes in your life. All it takes is a few negatives in order for one to go back to where they once were. I implore you if that happens to start again. Fight the urge to go back to your old ways. I know it is hard sometimes, but we really do make things in life much more difficult by assuming that they are more difficult, when in reality it is only our own independent thought that makes it this way. Remember you control your mind, and what you think is what it believes.

You have so much to do in life, and God wants you to do it <u>all</u>. Never give up on your hopes and dream even if it takes longer to accomplish them. Everyday you need to use your moments as stepping-stones to guide you to your destiny. Things happen, and plans go in the wrong direction; but you have the ability to change that. If you are not where you want to be in life, then start making those changes. Keep telling yourself that whatever it is you are doing right now is only a stepping-stone to greater things to come. This is how I managed to get through some very difficult times in my life.

We all have to make some difficult decisions in life, but realize it is for the greater good (our greater good). While dieting, I am cutting out some of my favorite foods for right now. For me it is difficult because they are my favorite foods. Yet, I know it won't be forever and right now they just don't play a part in my good health plan. I am so lucky that God gave us another gift that I am currently using, and that is the gift of will power. What a GREAT gift this is. I also must admit that at times it has been tough while dieting, but it is this gift that has kept me going. I tend to eat out at restaurants a lot, and I find myself not finishing what I ordered, because I am no longer hungry. I have trained myself to say... no more. I also pass up desert and I drink plenty of water every day. If not for the gift of will power I might have really struggled. Also, the fact that I already know that I will be thinner lets me imagine in my mind what I look like and keeps me going. You need to be the same way in everything you are trying to achieve in life.

Whatever it is you need to accomplish in life, no matter how tough it may seem, know that it is only a stepping-stone away. Giving up my favorite foods, is one of my stepping-stones to a better, healthier me. I am excited about it and it keeps me motivated. Staying excited about accomplishing your dreams should keep you motivated as well. Just remember these two words: stepping-stones, stepping-stones, stepping-stones. Got it? Good, now take that step...

To become one,
one must first become

Splinters

As you continue to progress in your search for self-discovery, it is important to recognize that there will be a few, what I like to call, splinters along the journey. Splinter is another word I use for obstacle. I always let people know that negatives are a part of life. It is how we deal with them that will set us apart from others.

Along your spiritual journey when these splinters occur, you need to take a step back and figure out the best solution to the problem. Never give up on your success of overcoming the splinter that is before you. The answer to resolving the situation, no matter what it is, is to look inside of you. Now I know there are a lot of bad scenarios in life, but the answer to solving those problems are within you (I promise). My answer to deciphering the splinter may be different than yours. Your answer will be the correct response that you need in that moment. In addition, it is also important to know that asking for input from others is a good thing. This will give you many points of view on taking care of whatever needs to be done and with this I am sure you will make the right the decision.

Even in the event that the answer you chose to correct the dilemma may have not worked out as you intended, it is the answer you needed at that exact time. Remember that everything happens for a reason. Therefore, whatever the outcome, that was the outcome that was always intended. Once again, you always have the opportunity before you to continue seeking the solution to the splinter (obstacle) that is before you. Do not concede defeat.

Continue on. For example, say you want to start a business, and you are in need of working capital. You go to the bank, and the bank tells you that whatever it is you are trying to do will not work. The bank then denies your loan application. Let me ask you this, do you stop right there and give up? Or do you continue on to the next bank. The answer is… you continue on.

A good story about that is the one of Colonel Harland Sanders. You may not know who he is, but I guarantee you know his company. Colonel Harland Sanders is the mastermind behind Kentucky Fried Chicken (KFC). It was his recipe for the chicken that made him famous. He tried to sell his product to numerous restaurants, but in turn received many rejections along the way. This did not stop the good colonel though. He persevered and kept going knowing that eventually someone would take on his recipe. Low and behold, one day it happened and the rest is history.

This is what you need to do when a splinter appears before you. You may be asking why I call problems splinters. The answer is simple. It is because if you have ever had a splinter, you don't quit working to get it out until it's out. That's what you need to do when faced with adversity. You need to keep working on solving the issues that are before you until they are resolved. Remember, some splinters may be right on top and easy to get out and some may be deep and require some effort. Either way, you need to keep doing whatever is necessary to straighten out whatever needs to be corrected. By doing so, you will remain on your path of self-discovery and splinter free.

To take flight like a butterfly,

one must first break free from
one's cocoon.

Emerge

This should be a main goal within your life, the goal to emerge, or arrive if you will. You need to start believing that you are so much more than you think you are at this very moment. You have so many abilities within you and even more that lie before you. Like a tool belt fastened to your waist, these abilities are the tools that are ready to help build your destiny. These tools are available to you twenty-four hours a day, three hundred and sixty-five days a year (three hundred and sixty-six during leap years). Whatever you may need, already know it is before you. Create the life that you have always imagined. Create you.

God has given you the greatest gift one could ever have imagined. You have been given the gift of breath. This gift is your acclamation of life. What you choose to do with it now stands before you. From here on out you now know that whatever decisions you make will put you on the path that you have created. From this path the rest of your life will be dictated. What will you be remembered for? Will people even know who you were? This is up to you. You can be remembered as someone who lived life to its fullest or as someone who never lived at all. Either outcome is up to you. I choose the first. I choose to be someone who has lived life to its fullest and in doing so has chosen to help others in the process.

It does not matter who you are, where you came from, your social status, rich or poor, fat or thin. What matters is that you did something, and in the end, you can look back and know that you lived the best life possible. Therefore, the goal of life is to *EMERGE* from wherever you are right now and to become someone who took on life headfirst and lived it for all it's worth. To finally emerge from an ordinary existence into an extraordinary existence, like a caterpillar to a butterfly, it is before you, and once again it is you. As you sit there reading this book, I hope you are imagining all the great things in life that you are now going to accomplish. But remember this, as you are beginning your new life, you must also help humanity in the process. We are all a part of humanity. Therefore, as I am helping you, you must help others emerge also. We need to work together as a world. We need to let others know that they have the same possibilities that we have. They need to know that they can live an incredible life and that God truly loves them. Today is your day to start making the decisions in your life to become the new you. I have shared with you many of my own stories and given you the gifts that I have received from God the universe. These are the same gifts He has given to you. Remember that knowledge is power, and you possess an infinite amount of it. God has given this gift to you and what you choose to do with it is up to you.

Even as that caterpillar emerges from its cocoon into a beautiful butterfly, you too will emerge into a beautiful life. A life filled with all your hopes and dreams realized. Your time for change starts now. Do not wait for life to happen, make life happen. I believe in my heart that you will accomplish whatever it is you want to accomplish. I already know this. Now it is time for you to know this. Take my words and make them a reality within your own life, but more importantly make them a reality in someone else's life too. Oh and one quick message just for you… Know that God the universe is proud of you and wants to congratulate you on your current and future happiness, so do I. Congratulations!

Live in the light, it burns eternally by the power of you.

Responsible Consciousness

I am asking you to do this one simple thing. In fact, you can do it right where you are. I am asking all of you to have "responsible consciousness". Responsible consciousness is the act of being accountable for one's own awareness. You, as a being, are accountable for your own realizations. Whatever it is you desire in life, you are only answerable to yourself for its completion. Whatever it is that you are yearning for all comes down to you.

It is so easy for people (me included at one time) to place the blame on others for our own life "malfunctions". We need to take responsibility within our own lives to ensure that whatever it is we are longing for, we are successful at achieving it. We need to have responsible consciousness in everything we do and say. You are now going to be living in a higher state of consciousness. This means that your state of being (while awake) will now be more aware of what is going on around you.

Whether you are trying to buy a car or even a house, know that the only one stopping you from achieving success in this area is you. Remember that living in a higher state of consciousness also means that you have a higher power in fulfilling any specific visions you may have for your life. That said, any manifestations that you are trying to create, also falls upon you and only you to create. You now have an amazing ability to become what you always knew you could be. Living in a responsible consciousness gives you total control of your destiny. As said in poker, you hold all the cards.

Being responsible for your own actions will play a large part in your new life. It is life affirming to most people. To others around you, you will appear to be more confident, dependable, trustworthy and reliable. These are all good qualities in a person and this person is you. By just taking control of your responsible consciousness, you are setting yourself up for some amazing life journeys. You will now be able to put things into a clearer perspective when viewing them. All these changes are coming to you because you have decided to take control of your life. Responsible Consciousness is just one more thing you can add to the ever-growing list of life changes you are presently making. I can already sense your awareness getting stronger. With your ability to create a successful life, know that anything is possible.

Abundance flows towards you, but to accept it one must only ask for it

Hopelessness? I don't think so!

As we continue to challenge each other today to become the best person we can, it is imperative that we continue to challenge ourselves at the same time. Taking chances or opportunities as I call them, is a major part of reorganizing who you are. You, God, and humanity need to be the main focal points within your life, and without each other, the prospects of recreating who you are become lowered.

The likelihood of becoming whatever it is you want to develop within your life becomes much greater if you face it with God the universe involved. No problem is too intense that a solution cannot be found and that solution is inside you. Along your journey of self-discovery you will always come upon situations that seem hopeless. Yet still somehow those situations seem to be conquerable. Why do you think this is? It's because you have changed your perspective on the situation. You have chosen to believe that in life there is nothing that cannot be achieved if you set your mind to it.

Over the years, many people have overcome some of the most mind-boggling situations. From health problems to finances, people always seem to find a way to triumph over what others thought impossible. Even in the event of probable death, people have overcome what even top doctors throughout the world have said was hopeless. Why? It's because the human spirit to succeed is more powerful than that of the will to fail. If right now you were given only months to live, would you not do all you could to find a way to prolong your life? Of course you would. From medications (including those that are untested) to unorthodox treatments in foreign lands, you would fight with every ounce of your body to become cured. This is what you need to do in your everyday life. Fight for everything you dream of. People tend to give up too fast, and therefore they never succeed in what they set out to accomplish in the first place.

Any situation is only hopeless when you have given in to that feeling of hopelessness. If you believe there is no way to overcome the situation before you, then you are right. You have just exclaimed to the universe that you have, dare I say it, given up. You have succumbed to what you believe was insurmountable. To that I say, "I DON'T THINK SO"! You are so much stronger than that. You have the ability to make changes to any situation at any given time. God has given this to you. Hopelessness is not a word in our vocabulary. It is a word only used by those who actually believe it to be true.

Take a stand for who you are as a person and look at your situation. If it seems that the odds are against you, then use that to your advantage and turn things around. Go a different direction. Look for the road less traveled. I know that you can do anything you put your mind to, so go ahead and put your mind to changing your life for the better. You'll be so glad you did.

Happiness stems from love
and love stems from happiness.

Eternally.

Happiness . . .

I wanted to be the first one to congratulate you on your newfound success. I know some of you are still working towards it, but I felt compelled to be the first to let you know that by just starting to change your life, you have already succeeded. Everything here after is just icing on the cake. Struggle is a word you will no longer use in your everyday life. You have come to a point in your life where there are no longer any cross roads, because all roads now lead to your happiness.

Take a deep breath, smile and continue your journey. I firmly believe that affirmation is extremely important to all of our endeavors in life. It is good to know that others have taken notice of your new direction. As you continue on the journey of the many successes you will soon come across, I ask that no matter what, you take time out of your day to look up to the sky, outstretch your arms and say thank you to life. Let God the universe know how much you appreciate this gift He has helped you create.

You are an exceptional person, with many more passageways to be found within yourself, and those passageways are there just waiting to be explored by you. Dig deeper within yourself and I promise you will find more hidden treasures. Remain curious about everything, but never forget to put you first. When you put you first, you are putting God first. Live life to its fullest and never regret your past. Look to your future and all the possibilities it holds before you. I am so proud that you have taken the first of many steps in your search for all that you are. Today is your day. Make the most of it, and never forget to help your brothers and sisters around the world. They have dreams too…

Imagination is the key that unlocks thought.

Ready, Set, A.C.T.I.O.N.

The ability for one person to reconnect with their life is incredible. For millions to do it is mind staggering. Nevertheless, this is what has been happening over thousands of years. It seems like more and more people are taking control of their own personal situations. What makes a person like Napoleon Hill or Tony Robbins any better than you? The answer is that they understand what it takes to turn a life around for the positive. But, does this make them any better than you? No. The difference between them and you is that they found their moment of clarity, and that is what it takes to live your life of destiny.

Sure, when we see people like Neale Donald Walsch, who is a New York Times best-selling author, and we think people like Walsch have it made, that's not always the case. You need to understand that a lot of the people you see talking about their own personal experiences had to go through some very tough situations. Now, I am not telling you that to succeed in life you need to be homeless or bankrupt. What I am telling you is that if you read more about some of these people, you will see they came from very difficult backgrounds just like some of us. The only difference is when times got tough they took action.

As you may know, I love to take words and break them down to their simplest forms. In this case I have taken the word action and broken it down to the following:

A: Acquire: Acquire the knowledge necessary to accomplish whatever it is you want to achieve. Have a plan of action!

C: Communicate: Here is where most people tend to "fall off the horse". You need to communicate with others about your plans. Let them know what's going on in your life. Explain to them what you are going to be doing and how you are going to do it.

T: Time: Give whatever it is you are doing some time to work. You may see results right away, but in most cases it may take some time, so be patient!

I: Initiate: Initiate your plans. Don't just sit back and wait for things to happen. Make them happen. You will see results much sooner.

O: Opportunities: Every day you have the opportunity to do whatever you want to do in life. You need to seize each and every one of them. Opportunities come and go quickly, so you need to grab as many as possible.

N: Never give up: We do not fail, we learn. So if you don't see results instantly, or you are struggling to continue, keep going anyway. It is better to look back at your life and know that you tried and succeeded, than to look back and know that you gave up on yourself. On a personal note, this was my problem with dieting. I would start and stop over and over again. Then I would imagine where I would have been had I not given up initially. Trust me on this one. Never give up; just keep moving forward!

So what is the plan for your life? Do you have one? If not, this would be a good time to start setting one up and putting it into action. Your life is yours to live, and how you choose to live it is in your hands. Your actions today will dictate how you live tomorrow.

Thoughts won't change your life.
It's putting those thoughts
into action
that will change your life!

Simple Reflections

You can really tell a lot about a person by just looking into their eyes. It is said that the eyes are the windows into a person's soul, and I believe that. Have you ever looked into the eyes of someone and just instantly known what was going on in that person's life? Well, the same can be said about someone looking into your eyes. When someone gazes into your eyes what do you think he or she will see? Will someone see happiness or will someone see a troubled soul? It really depends on how you are living your life.

Here is a quick experiment to help you see what others are seeing. Take a moment and stand in front of a mirror and look directly into your own eyes. Do not drift off and look at only one eye at a time. It is important that you look straight ahead and see both eyes. What do you see? Stay there for a few moments and continue to study what you are seeing in your reflection. This is how many people will evaluate you as a person. What you see is what others see. Your eyes are a reflection of your life. They tell stories to others about who and what you are. They tell stories of where you have been and where you are going. What stories are your eyes telling?

When you look into the mirror and see this simple reflection looking back at you, how do you feel? Are you happy or sad? Are you seeing the real you for the very first time? When I did this straightforward experiment for the first time, I saw pain and heartache in my eyes. I saw a man who looked like life had beaten him down. If I saw this, then I knew that others around me were seeing the very same thing, if not worse. I knew I had to make some changes in my life if I was to ever get that look out of my eyes. As I started to make minimal changes for the positive within my own life, I would look into the mirror to see if the image was also changing, and it was.

What I found out from this experiment is that even the simplest of adjustments in my own life would make very dramatic changes in my eyes. I noticed if I was upset about something my eyes would show it. When I started to make positive changes, my eyes reflected those changes. I also noticed that when I smiled more it made a huge impact on how my eyes seemed to react to it. I realized that who I was as a person, was exposed through my eyes.

How many times have you looked at someone and thought to yourself that this person is a lost soul? I know I have far too many times. People can interpret your mood from just a simple glance into your eyes. What happens when they have a longer view into them? Now is the time to look into your eyes and to see what others are seeing. If changes need to be made, you will know. A life that is filled with inner peace and harmony will tend to have a sparkle in the eyes. This should be the ultimate goal for all of us in our simple reflections.

Don't waste time waiting for things to happen, create them now.

Your happiness depends on it.

The Moment

Here it is, the moment of truth. Remember, God the universe is always supporting you. You have been created to live the most astonishing life possible. This was set forth by God the universes own creation, the creation of you. Whatever you choose to do with your life from this point on, know that you are in total control of it. At no point during your life, can you or will you ever be without God. God will be with you at all times. One must understand this truth in order to remain on the path of personal self-discovery and inevitability one's own enlightenment.

He who understands that life was created by a higher power, that power being God the universe, is the one who will succeed in accomplishing what has been set forth into motion by their creation. You were designed exactly the way you are for a specific purpose (reason). The nature of your design is one of complexity, but also one that holds all universal truths. Through the innovation, that is your soul, God has given you all that you will ever need to create what was created for you.

Each one of Gods creations holds a part of what is, was and ever will be. It is not by coincidence that you are here. It is by the correlation of many things including Gods precise timing that you are living in this exact moment. Look around and see all that you have created for yourself. It is not by accident, chance or a twist of fate that this has happened. Everything you have ever done or said throughout your entire existence has brought you to this exact point within your own moment. Those that have faith within God and themselves will understand this. Those that don't will have yet to realize the true potential they have within themselves.

For those who are still seeking their own enlightenment, it is at an exact moment in time when your clarity will become your reality. It is at this point that you will have reached absolute completeness with your soul, thus confirming to the universe and beyond, that you are one with all. No singular vibration from ones reality ever goes un-noticed within the vast expansion of that which is. It is through these vibrations that one even exists.

As time progresses your awareness will become more familiar, and it is at this point when goals and objectives can be achieved. The subject of life is not merely to live it on the surface, but to break through your mind, body and soul. It is through these three divine operating systems that the origin of your creation began. As you continue to exist, because of the creative process of all three systems, you will finally understand life and its origins. No man shall ever know the true meaning of life until he understands the true meaning of himself.

Your voyage into destiny will transport you to many places throughout the realm of all that is possible. The possible exists because of man's belief within himself.

Question: Is it through these beliefs that one can truly understand the continuation of his or her very own existence? The answer is yes.

Belief will play a key role in knowing who and what you are as a being. It is the intricate formations of your own awareness that continues to bring you to the edge of knowing. Knowing all that is, was, and ever will be.

Placed within you by God Himself is "all". All is every part of creation that exists within you, and because of this you are a complete being. There is nothing that God has not brought into your mind, body, and soul that does not explain the basis of your very own creation. Without these gifts you would live in a world of complete nothingness. As a life form this would make man lifeless or obsolete in fulfilling his or her purpose, and man was created for a purpose.

The faith that one carries throughout his journey and his eventual enlightenment, will be another key to the many successes that lie before him. As I said earlier, one must possess only two things to succeed in life. The first is to believe in God and oneself, and the second is to have faith in both. These two key elements, belief and faith, will eventually bring man to the third key element of life, the element of hope. This is the element that continues to keep man going in a forward direction. The hope that one day man will have a better understanding of himself and the possibilities that are before him.

One day you will understand who you are. When that day comes, you will also understand that as a part of creation itself, the possibilities for your life are endless. This is not just any other moment in your life, the moment when you finally realize all that you are. It is the moment in your life when you truly begin to live. It is the moment of you.

Life is like hitting a baseball.
The more contacts you make,
the better your average
for success becomes.

Listening to Society

Please read these next few words very carefully. Do not always listen to what society says! Did you read them carefully? If not, let me say it again: do not always listen to what society says. We are a world who tends to believe everything we hear that pertains to us personally; things like beauty, money, success, and so forth are things that pertain to us personally. Let me explain...

Society seems to have a "standard" definition for what the above mentioned things are. We are supposed to look a certain way to be considered beautiful or we need to have a certain amount of money or certain job to be considered successful. Forget all that, right now! That is not the reality or true definition of what any of those really are. The true definition of all those are set by you and not society. If I was to follow what society says, I would not be considered truly successful right now, and I would definitely not fall into what society deems to be beautiful.

What do I do since I do not fall into society's description of these things? The truth? I could care less about what society thinks and you should be the same way. We are all beautiful and we all have different ideas of success. Some of the most successful people I know make very little money, but are the happiest people I have ever met. Success is not about money. Success is about what brings you happiness. For me I am successful if I can help just one person doing what I do. Since I have been blessed to help many, I consider myself a success.

As for beauty? I am the most beautiful me I know and you are the most beautiful you! I understand that society defines beauty by ridiculous standards, but that is to sell products. We as a society need to learn to be comfortable in our own skin. We need to stop listening to what "society" says and begin to live our own life with our own definition of beauty and success. If you can do that, you are perfect and never forget that.

Before We Go . . .

What happens when our physical bodies die? Where do we go? Do we even go anywhere? The answers to these questions can once again be found deep within your soul. Remember you are an eternal being. Although your physical body will die and become dust, your spiritual body will live on forever.

We, as beings always seem to fear the inevitable. We look at death and fear what will happen when we must face it. We fear because we do not know what will happen on the other side of life, and that is exactly what it is, the other side of life. We need to take fear out of the equation because fear does not exist. We as beings have two sides. The first is the physical realm and the second is the spiritual realm. Each realm holds its own distinct virtues. In the physical realm we have the ability to see only what is before us. In the spiritual realm, we will have the ability to see and be all that is before, during and after our own existence. Just as God is in everything, so shall you be. Death is not to be feared, but to be appreciated.

Everyone has a place and time already planned out when the death of their physical bodies will occur. At that exact moment in time, one will then be moved into the spiritual realm of his life and that, my friend, is eternal. As for any fears you may have let me say this: With God there is no fear. There is only truth, and the truth is you are a creation of God the universe. You are a part of God himself, and God fears nothing. With God there is no fear. Does that make sense to you? God did not create you to live this one and only existence. He created you to live an eternal existence.

As time continues and you become more and more aware of your spiritual side, you will begin to understand this phase of your life. Also note that what you do in the physical world will carry over into the spiritual world. It is allied Karma. Karma follows you at all times of your life. Whether it is your earthly phase or your spiritual phase, karma is and always will be with you. I don't really like to call the end of my physical body "death". I prefer to call it my new life phase - a transition if you will. Unfortunately the word death has a very negative stigma attached to it. People associate it with the finality of life. I associate it with the beginning of a new life.

Through one's own physical death a new beginning is formed, and from that new beginning an entirely new aspect of your life begins. The key word here is life. Yes, a new life will begin and you will emerge from your body just as that butterfly emerges from its cocoon to start its new journey. You will become new in all its glory. You will rise from what you once were, to become what you forever will be. Yes, physical death is inevitable, but it is not the end of your life. It is just a new start in all that God has created. It will be through this new start, that you will finally understand the true power of God the universe.

Here's some investment advice...
Invest in yourself...

It pays the highest dividends!

Random Acts of Kindness

I couldn't finish this book without adding Random Acts of Kindness. This is incredibly significant in recreating who and what you are as a being. This is where you truly start using your new gifts. What is a Random Act of Kindness? It is just what it says it is. It is the act of doing something kind for others without expecting anything in return. I am sure daily you receive these acts, but never really noticed. Today, all of that changes. Today you will not only notice these acts, but you will also start to do them yourself. Random Acts of Kindness do not have to be financial. They can be as simple as a smile.

Below I have listed fifteen acts. This number is nothing to the many possibilities that are before you. These are just a few to get you started. Of the fifteen on the list, I have personally done all of them at some point and time. Now it is your turn to add to the list. Start today. Once you do, you will never stop.

1. Open a door for someone
2. Buy flowers for someone
3. Send someone a card
4. Visit someone you don't know in the hospital
5. Buy lunch for the car behind you in the drive thru
6. Pick up another tables bill at a restaurant
7. Offer to walk your neighbor's dog
8. Let someone cut in front of you in line
9. Write a letter to someone looking for help

10. Give up your parking space to someone else
11. Help someone finish a project
12. Run an errand for someone
13. Help someone in need
14. Help someone change a flat tire
15. Give somebody a hug

Remember there are endless possibilities for you to do. Start your own list and work through them on a daily basis. At the end of the month, start all over again. The feeling of doing something for someone else is incredible and it will make that person's day. Then again, it will probably make yours too. This is just another way to help you recreate yourself into becoming the person you have always known you would be.

Let your mind wander,
there are many places your
thoughts haven't been yet

Free Spirit

Oh what a feeling to be a free spirit in this world; to be free of all the bondages of everyday life. Today you set yourself on that path. The path of a new you, controlled only by you. How great is that! So what is a free spirit? A free spirit is a person who lives life with extreme intensity. They let nothing get in the way of what they want out of life. They enjoy every moment and never let the little things bother them. They control their own destiny. A destiny where boundaries are forbidden and challenges excite them.

Are you this person? If not, you're on your way. This is what life is all about. It's about taking on the challenges of a new day with the perspective of living a carefree life. No matter where you are at in your personal journey, you need to start living in the moment of now. Each day will bring new questions, however as a creation of God the universe you already have the answers that you are looking for to respond to those questions. A free spirit knows this and continues to move forward unabated by any negatives. They live to live, and not merely to just get by.

The next question is "How does one become a free spirit?" The answer is simple. You don't become a free spirit, because you are a free spirit. This is already instilled with in you. It is another one of God's countless gifts to you. Let me say that again. You already are a free spirit. You just have to open your mind to the experience and the possibility that anything is possible. Know that life will not pass you by, and that you will live it to the fullest with no excuses or regrets. Doing so will bring out this gift, the gift of the free spirit.

My friend, I am so excited to share this information with you. I struggled so long in my life until I was able to unlock these gifts within myself. They have given me a new perspective on life. It allows me to be me. I can be whomever I choose to be. Free spirits are not looking for the approval of their peers. They are doing what they believe is best for them, and that is to enjoy life. There are always going to be negative people in the world who will do whatever it takes to destroy other people's dreams. However, it is those who look at life in an entirely different way that will always rise above and succeed against those naysayers. These people are the true free spirits. For they live life not a day at a time nor even an hour, but a moment at a time.

It is time for you rise up from the ashes that were once you and shout out to the universe that you are a free spirit. You are no longer the person you used to be. No more living other people's dreams. It is time to start living yours, perhaps for the first time. Make today the day you declare your free spirit. Remember this gift is already inside of you. It is up to you to release this power, and once you do the future is yours.

To be one with the Universe
is to be one with God.

Did You Know?

Who is God? What is God? Does God even exist? These questions have beleaguered man for centuries. I can tell you this, God does exist and He exists in the form of you. Yes, you. You are a part of God. We all have the same Creator. We were all created by the one who created all that is, was, and ever will be. This means that you are a part of the original creation of life and everything else that will ever be created.

People still question the existence of God, because they have yet to realize what or who they are, and what or who they are is a part (or extension) of God. You have the capability to do what others have done before you for centuries: to live the most astonishing life possible. God created you for a reason, and that reason is for you to initiate your own sense of reality. You are here to create your own destiny. You are here to establish your life. You are here as a part of God to create what will exist for eternity.

When you were created, God also created something for you called your soul. What is your soul? Once again, your soul is the epicenter of who you are. In simpler terms it is you. It is a living entity that is within you. It contains all that was, is and ever will be created by the hand of God. You have within you the entire mainframe of life itself, a biological and spiritual wonder. Through your soul you are able to connect with every part of your being. Through your soul you are able to connect with everything that is around you. The hand of God connects us all and it is through our souls that we make this connection.

Some people will say that we are not a part of God nor can one connect with their soul. The reason people say things like this is they have yet to truly connect with God on a one to one basis, or they have yet to unite with their own soul. To connect with your soul, you must believe that this connection is possible. Billions of people over the centuries have experienced both a one on one connection with God and with their soul. This connection does exist. It exists in every one of us. It is through these connections that we have the potential to live the most incredible lives. It is through these connections that one even exists. It is through these connections that you yourself are present within your own being.

Set your sights high in life. Don't just settle for an "ordinary" existence, because that was not Gods intentions for you when you were created. You are here at this exact moment in time for a specific reason and it is up to you to find out what that reason is. The answer is within you. It is within your soul. Make the connection today and start to live a life of abundance sent forth from God Himself just for you. The connection you and God share is not just some random phenomenon. It is a critical part of your existence.

In life, each of us will have a different mechanism within us that will lead us to our soul connection. Each occurrence with your soul will keep you on the path to your destiny. Ask the questions and receive the answers. Your soul is the very essence of you and all that you will create within your own existence. Use your soul as a guide that will lead you to fulfilling your dreams. Discover all that God has created for you and all that you have created for yourself. As a part of God you have the power to do this. You have this power (gift), because you are a part of God Himself.

Sometimes the end is just the beginning.

One with God the Universe . . .

I am not a miracle worker, healer, life coach or whatever term may encompass that which is not me. I am a believer. I am a believer in humanity. I believe in humanity's ability to overcome any obstacles set before them, if they choose to do so. I believe in humanity's insatiable desire to be the best at whatever they set their mind to. I also believe in man's ability for compassion towards his fellow man. Therefore, I am a believer and being a believer means I believe in you too.

I believe that whatever stands before you, no matter how big the task, can be accomplished by you. It's not me I need to convince of your God given abilities, but you. You need to know how truly special you are. You need to know that God created you for a purpose. That purpose, though it may not seem perfect right now for some, is not to suffer, but to live the best life possible. No one person can accomplish anything in their lifetime without the assistance of those around them. No one person can accomplish anything in their lifetime without having a connection with God, whether they choose to believe that or not. God is always with you. You do not have to believe in God to have a connection with Him, because your connection was already established at your creation. Whether you choose to interact with Him or not, He continually interacts with you. Thus giving you the power to create the life you choose. However, I am a believer, and I believe a better life comes to fruition when we build a strong connection with the God the universe.

God has placed before you many other beings. As you look around you will see the many faces of your brothers and sisters. Though your brothers and sisters may look different than you, we are all still one. Together we can achieve anything. Apart, we achieve nothing. So look around at humanity. See the big picture God has presented before you. Look to the heavens and outstretch your arms and know that God the universe is reaching out to embrace you. Feel the warmth of His touch. Know love as you have never known it before. Know the truth of Gods unconditional love. It does not matter who you are or where you came from, you are a creation of God.

As a creation of God, it is your destiny to be all that one can be. Remember that Jesus, Buddha and many others are creations of God also, so you are related to some great people. Stand with pride. Stand with your head held high. Stand, just stand and know that forever you will be one with humanity and know that you will forever be one with God and all that has ever been created.

To settle in life is to say
that you have finished living.

God's Spiritual Network
(The power of the Universe)

I wanted to share with you another one of my many moments with God. Remember we all have them, but only a few realize and believe this to be true. Anyway here's what happened…

At one of my old jobs I made friends with a person who I had a lot in common with. At work we would talk endlessly about life and God. We had many great discussions and in the end became good friends. Anyway, as fate would have it, I eventually moved from that city to another some 1200 miles away. Although we stayed in touch, usually by email, the emails became less and less frequent.

Now you have to understand this part. Although we emailed back and forth over the span of about twelve months, we never talked on the phone or saw each other since I moved. That said, one day out of the blue, God told me to call this person. He said I needed to speak with him. Then without hesitation, I called my friend up. Unfortunately he did not answer, but I left a message. I told him that God told me to call you today and that whatever you are going through know that God is with you….

I didn't hear from my friend for another week or so and when he did contact me it was by email. He told me that he appreciated the call and it came at the right time. He told me that I called at 6:21 p.m., and his father passed away at 7:00 p.m. thirty-nine minutes later. I believe God wanted me to call my friend to help put his mind at ease and let him know that God was in control; and that everything was going to be all right.

My friend went on to say that he was with his dad when he passed, and his dad went peacefully. His description of his father's passing mirrored that of my brother, who was with my mom when she passed. In the end this brought comfort to my friend's heart, and established the fact that we are all connected through God's spiritual network.

As you have inspired me,
I hope I have inspired you.

Oh, one last thing . . .

Remember you are never on your journey alone. God plays essential roles in all you do. Without Him this book really is just words on a page. Also, even though you are in total control of your destiny, make contacts and use them. Contacts are people that have been brought into your life for a reason. It is not that they may have something for you to know; it is that they *do* have something for you to know. Like I wrote earlier, we all need to share the knowledge that we have. It's not just because I took control of my destiny that I am finally starting to live the life that I always knew I would. It is also because of the contacts that were brought into my life.

Well, here we are at the end of the book, but once again not the journey. I have one last thing for you to do. After reading this book I want you to sit back and think for a moment about your life. I want you to think of everything - the good and the bad. Then below I want you to write who you used to be as a person. Then on the lines following that, I want you to write who you are now as a person. Remember after reading this book and implementing it into your life, you are no longer the person you once were. You are now in the process of becoming the person you always knew you would be.

I want to thank you again for being such an amazing inspiration to me and to the world. I am so excited about all the possibilities that are now before you. We all have choices in life and now you have some more knowledge that will help guide you along the way. Life is for living. Life is meant for enjoying and sharing. It is meant to be everything you ever imagined it could be. Now because of you, it will be. Enjoy your life, but more importantly enjoy each and every moment of it.

We all have great lives in store for us, and I wish you all pleasant travels on your journey.

Who I used to be

_____

_____

_____

_____

_____

_____

_____

Who I am Now!

_____

_____

_____

_____

_____

_____

_____

_____

_____

The Blank Page

I always like to add a little something special at the end of my books to help you kick-start your new life. This time it is all about you and nobody else. Enjoy…

Life is like writing a book. Before you stand's a blank page, and what that page will eventually entail is up to you. The story you write will contain every aspect of your life in specific detail. All the highs and all the lows will be visible for the entire world to see. Keeping that in mind, you have the opportunity to create one of the most amazing adventure stories ever told in the history of mankind - a story that will be read and re-read throughout history. You have been given this gift of a blank page, so you can tell your story in your own words and not somebody else's.

How will your story begin? I have left a few blank pages at the end of this book on purpose. Since you have now read this book, you have the knowledge to create one of the most amazing life stories ever told. What you write is up to you and you alone. I have no doubts about how wonderful your story will be. Live life to its fullest, but don't forget to write. Keep that story going, and in the end you'll look back and smile, because you will have lived your life on your terms. No regrets, no if only – just, I did. What an impressive account of your life it will be. The world looks forward to reading it, but you will have had the pleasure of living it. We too will live it. We will live it through you and your existence.

It is time to pick up that pen and to start writing. Today

you begin a new life and a new story. Remember I don't write chapters in my books, I write in moments. I hope you will do the same. Write each and every moment for all it is worth. Never give up and know the world eagerly awaits the story of you.

Thank You Page

To everyone that is, was and ever will be, I say thank you...

A letter to you...

I wanted to finish this book with a thank you to you personally. As you continue on your journey of self-discovery, I wanted to ask you a few questions.

You have worked hard your entire life to get to this exact moment in time. Are you where you want to be at in life? Are you happy? If not, where do you go from here?

The Dalai Lama said: *"The purpose of life is to be happy."* How true that is. The problem with most people not being happy is quite simple. The reason is that they see their flaws. I talked about flaws earlier in this book (Veer off the Beaten Path). The dictionary defines a flaw as this: A feature that mars perfection of something. Well, that is the problem. We are all trying to be perfect in our lives, when in reality it is our "flaws" that make us who we are. Therefore, how do we overcome this problem?

The answer is... we don't. While meditating one day I asked God to help guide me to an answer to this problem so many of us seem to be having. This is the answer I received:

Flaws are what make things beautiful. Without them everything would be exactly the same. Flaws create individuality and individuality creates you. With all the strife of the outside world, it is important to look inward and live from a perspective of love. In order to obtain that which you are seeking in your existence, you must find love always within. It is only then, when you find this love, that all things will become perfect just as they are.

Today I am asking that when life becomes more difficult than you can handle to look within yourself and find that love. Find the flaw that makes you who you are and *Find Love Always Within.*

Peace, Joy, Love & Abundance,
Rick

www.RickDorociak.com

This Is Where
Your Dreams Begin